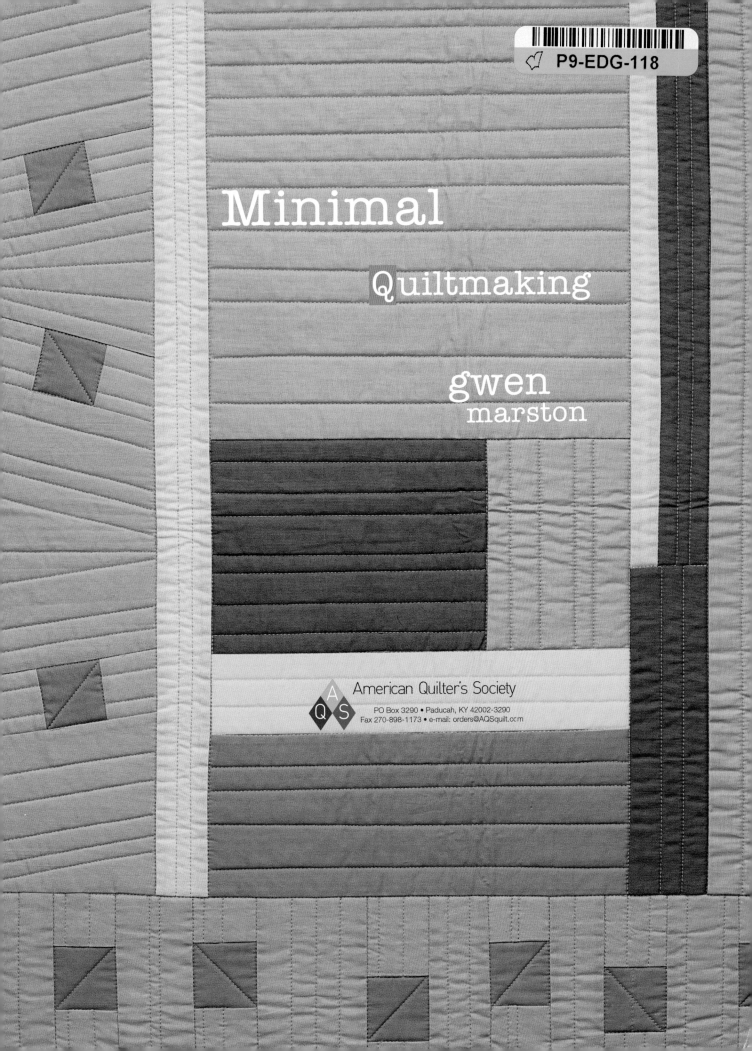

Minimal

Quiltmaking

gwen
marston

American Quilter's Society

PO Box 3290 • Paducah, KY 42002-3290
Fax 270-898-1173 • e-mail: orders@AQSquilt.com

Located in Paducah, Kentucky, the American Quilter's Society (AQS) is dedicated to promoting the accomplishments of today's quilters. Through its publications and events, AQS strives to honor today's quiltmakers and their work and to inspire future creativity and innovation in quiltmaking.

EXECUTIVE BOOK EDITOR: ELAINE H. BRELSFORD
SENIOR BOOK EDITOR: LINDA BAXTER LASCO
COPY EDITOR: JOANN TREECE
PROOFREADER: CHRYSTAL ABHALTER
GRAPHIC DESIGN: ELAINE WILSON
COVER DESIGN: MICHAEL BUCKINGHAM
QUILT PHOTOGRAPHY: CHARLES R. LYNCH
HOW-TO PHOTOGRAPHY: GWEN MARSTON

Additional copies of this book may be ordered from the American Quilter's Society, PO Box 3290, Paducah, KY 42002-3290, or online at www.AmericanQuilter.com.

Text © 2014, Author, Gwen Marston
Artwork © 2014, American Quilter's Society

American Quilter's Society

PO Box 3290 • Paducah, KY 42002-3290
Fax 270-898-1173 • e-mail: orders@AQSquilt.com

Library of Congress Control Number: 2014935196

COVER: WINTER BEECH, detail. Full quilt on page 56.

TITLE PAGE: SPLIT PEA, detail. Full quilt on page 61.

OPPOSITE: MINIMAL IN NEUTRALS, detail. Full quilt on page 52.

Dedication

~~~~~~~~~~~

I dedicate this book to all the quilters who have come to my lectures and classes and who have bought my books for years. Without you, chances are I probably wouldn't have published nearly as many. Thank you.

And as an elder in the quilt world, I also dedicate this book to the new generation of quilters. I admire their spunk, welcome them with enthusiasm, and trust them to carry the future of quiltmaking forward.

Acknowledgments

With this book, I have published nine books with AQS and I thank them for having confidence in me and making it possible to share my ideas about quilts.

I thank my editors, Elaine Brelsford and Linda Baxter Lasco, for their always helpful and wise advice, and I thank Ginny Harris who kept all of us on track.

Twenty-two of my friends from across the country generously allowed me to include their work in this book, for which we all are grateful. Their well articulated views of what goes into a Minimal quilt added an indispensable flavor to this book that makes it all the more tasty. Thank you, girls.

Elisa Albury
Deb Albright
Kathleen Awalt
Pam Beal
Nancy Caleshu
Rogene Fischer
Kathleen Glynn
Pat Haas
Lynn Harris
Pat Isaman
Cathy Jones
Barbara Mars
Nancy Perkins
Jan Rajeck
Judy Rantz
Joanne Salz
Kathy Sandling
Kristin Shields
Phyllis Small
Jan Tetzlaff
Marge Tucker
Carol Van Sickle

MINIMAL IN LAVENDER, RED, AND GREEN, detail. Full quilt on page 35.

Table of Contents

6   Introduction

11   How to Use This Book

12   About Designing

16   Minimal Quilts

34   Hard-Edge Quilts

49   Minimal Color

66   Minimal Quilts Inspired by Art

77   Gallery

89   The Grand Finale: A Baker's Dozen

94   About the Author

95   Other Books by Gwen Marston

ORANGE ON WHITE, detail. Full quilt on page 48.

Introduction

I n the early 1970s, I discovered quiltmaking, answered the call, and began my life as a quiltmaker. Today, I am as passionate about making quilts as I was with that first quilt. As one should expect, I've gone through different stages in my work, and the quilts I make today differ from the quilts made in earlier periods. Still, I have been living with Modernism tossed in with primitive for many years, and when I look over my shoulder, I see my early influences following close behind.

In the 1700s, long before the term "minimal art" made its debut, American women were turning out wholecloth quilts using unprinted fabrics with no piecing or appliqué. These quilts were also made in France, England, Wales, and probably other countries, too. If you apply the definition of minimalism, "any design or style in which the simplest and fewest elements are used to create the maximum effect," it seems these quilts might surely be considered "minimal." Most often they were white, and are now referred to as "all white quilts." They also came in indigo blue, watermelon pink, bright yellow, olive green, apricot, and red. Their common distinguishing feature was the quilting—elegant designs, often organic, and, it would appear, always coupled with intellectual rigor.

From the beginning, I was drawn to quilts that were shockingly sparse and breathtakingly beautiful. I found them in books like *America's Quilts and Coverlets* (Carleton Safford and Robert Bishop, Weathervane Books, 1974); and *New Discoveries in American Quilts* (Robert Bishop, E.P. Dutton, 1975). I found them in *The Quilt Engagement Calendars,* which were full of fine antique quilts lovingly compiled by Cyril Nelson (E.P. Dutton,

1975–2001). I have relied so heavily on Cyril's calendars for so long that I pretty well have them memorized. I will be sitting upstairs looking out the window, thinking about quilts, when one of my favorites comes to mind. I can go downstairs, stand in front of my bookcase looking at my calendars, and come within one or two years of guessing which one contains the quilt I want to study again. And I happen to know that I'm not the only one of my generation who can do this.

Speaking of *The Quilt Engagement Calendars,* the idea for CUT-OUT CORNERS (right) is from a c.1820 New England quilt shown in the 1985 calendar (Plate 50, should you happen to have it in your own library). It left a lasting impression on me and 23 years later I set about making my own version using the timeless design ideas from that first quilt made some 185 years earlier. I think the design ideas in the original quilt are as strong and fresh as the day it came out of the quilt frame and went onto the bed. It exemplifies the power of minimal design and the remarkable longevity of good design.

CUT-OUT CORNERS, 45" × 45", 2005.
Made and hand quilted by the author.

Gwen at home. Photo by Frank Solle.

CENTER DIAMOND, 72" x 72", 1982. Designed, made, and hand quilted by the author.

Later influences were Lancaster Amish quilts with their simple graphic designs and bold colors. These were the first quilts to be taken seriously as art, when in 1971 Amish quilts from the Jonathan Holstein and Gail van der Hoof collection were shown at the Whitney Museum of Art in New York. They were seen as art. At the time, they caused as big a stir as the Gee's Bend quilts later caused when first shown in June 2006 at the Museum of Fine Arts, Houston.

In 1982, I made my first Amish-style quilt inspired by the one on the cover of Robert Bishop and Elizabeth Safanda's *A Gallery of Amish Quilts: Design Diversity from a Plain People* (E.P. Dutton, 1976). With unbridled enthusiasm, I made the top and figured out how to mark it with traditional Amish designs that were new to me. Once marked and in the frame, I hand quilted this first CENTER DIAMOND (left and below) in ten days. I remember it well

because it was a memorable accomplishment. I stuck right with it because I couldn't wait to see it finished.

These Amish quilts and the sparse quilts I mentioned earlier might well be considered "minimal." In fact, the late *New York Times* art critic Robert Hughes called Lancaster County Amish women "the creators of the first modern abstract art in America." See where I'm going with this?

Having explored a number of different styles of quilts, I have found myself drifting back to old loves—simple, sparse quilts. You will see some of this work in my last four books: *Liberated Medallion Quilts* (AQS, 2012); *37 Sketches* (Six Mile Press, 2011); *Liberated Quiltmaking II* (AQS, 2009); and *Ideas and Inspirations: Abstract Quilts in Solids* (MoCa Press, 2008).

As with minimal art, the focus of designing minimal quilts is to produce work that has been reduced to its essence—stripped down to its essentials. Mies van der Rohe, regarded as one of the masters of modern design and architecture, was fond of saying "less is more." He is also associated with the phrase "God is in the details."

To my eye, most often the simplest designs are the most pleasing, the most sophisticated and exciting. I think it's also true that when design is stripped down to its rudiments, when there is in fact "less," everything counts more. What I have found in my design work is that when there is less, I have to work harder to make a composition work.

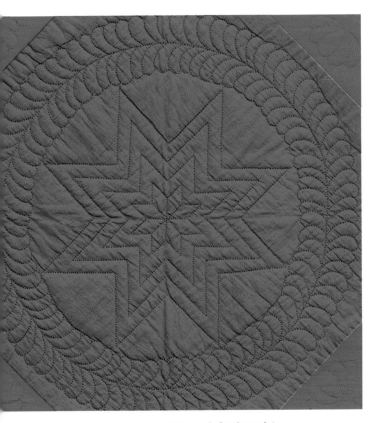

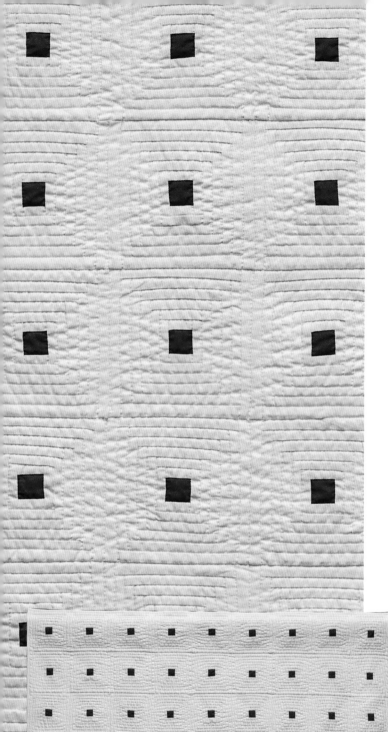

Introduction

Nancy Caleshu's RED CENTERS (left) is an American classic artfully transformed into a stunning and sophisticated minimal quilt. As this quilt demonstrates, a sense of beauty and calmness often comes with simplicity and order. Texture and shadows formed by the seam lines and quilting are effective features appropriate to a minimal quilt such as this.

A Word About the Quilts

The recently made quilts shown in this book were all made with the intention of making new work consistent with the principles of minimal art. Minimal art grew out of Modernism, so there is naturally an overlapping of the two styles. For example, while the modern artist Mark Rothko was generally identified as an Abstract Expressionist, many of his paintings seem to fit the definition of minimal art. (He himself rejected being classified as an abstract painter, so I risk sounding audacious by suggesting his work seems minimal.)

As the author, I made the decision to use a broad definition of minimalism rather than adhering to the stricter definition. Art is sometimes hard to categorize and even artists themselves differ with the art critics about where their own work fits. The truth of the matter is that "minimal" means different things to different people and you see that delightfully reflected in these quilts.

LEFT: RED CENTERS, 46" x 46", 2013. Designed, made, and hand quilted by Nancy Caleshu, Lopez Island, Washington.

How to Use This Book

What I have been trying to do in my classes and my writings over the years is to share ideas that help quilters find their own path to making the quilts unique to themselves. My job description, which I wrote myself, is to show quilters practical ways to figure things out for themselves, and to provide tips on solving design and construction problems. Looking back over years of quiltmaking and teaching, it occurs to me that knowing how to get yourself out of trouble is an essential skill for the proficient quilter to acquire. "Painting yourself into a corner" happens to all of us; so knowing how to get out is mightily advantageous.

In this book you will notice that instead of patterns, I offer a process. I will tell you how I constructed the various parts of my quilts so you can make your own parts, and because you are using a *process* instead of a *pattern,* your quilt will be your own original design. There is power in that. It's rewarding and affirming. My roots are very much from the tradition of quiltmaking and a time when many quilters were working in this same process-focused way.

Looking back at how American women made their quilts in earlier times, there is a lot of evidence that they were making their own decisions about what and how to make their quilts and that they favored practical solutions to design and construction problems. We Americans like to think of ourselves as being known for our ingenuity. Out on the farm there wasn't anyone to ask, so people found ingenious solutions to everyday problems including quiltmaking problems. And it's truly easier than you might think. All the classes I teach revolve around giving quilters the tools they need to design and make their own quilts and I have found that the vast majority of the students in my classes have been successful.

As you experiment with the construction techniques I offer, remember that there are lots of ways to do almost everything, and I encourage you to alter my ideas to suit yourself. One size does not fit all, and it's up to each of us to find the way we prefer to work. If you have an easier way to do something, be my guest.

You will enjoy your work more and do a better job if you are working within your own comfort zone. As I have often said, "None of us is making quilts to add just a little more stress to our lives."

About Designing

As I begin this discussion with you about designing, I want to say that there are many ways to go about it. I work out my ideas in a number of different ways that I'll touch on here.

In 1981, I sewed the leftovers from a full-size quilt into a doll quilt measuring about 18" x 20". I've continued to make doll-size quilts and now have well over 400 of them filling many drawers in my house. Looking back, I think making these small pieces helped me develop my own artistic aesthetics more than almost anything I've done. Working small allows me to experiment with more ideas and be more adventuresome because there is less risk in both time and expense.

From the beginning of my interest in quilts, I looked to antique quilts for design clues, finding them to be more interesting artistically than the new work being done in the traditional style. One of the artistic ideas I noticed, took to heart, and use to this day, was color substitution in both block construction and wholecloth pieced borders. Chances are it was because the quilter ran out of material and simply made do with what was available, but whatever the reason, I thought it made the quilt less predictable and therefore, more interesting. I felt that the asymmetrical pieced sections added to the artistic success of a quilt and this idea has become a standard in my work. I've used it in traditional quilts to make them look more authentically "traditional." And I've dragged it into the twenty-first century and used it to make quilts with a contemporary look.

Discovering what I now call "Liberated quiltmaking" was the changing point for me; because once I had that, I felt I could figure out how to make anything I wanted. From that point on, experimental construction became a major focus in my work. With this new-found discovery I started looking at everything differently and I've shared many of these ideas in three books published by the American Quilter's Society: *Liberated Quiltmaking* (1996), *Liberated Quiltmaking II* (2009), and *Liberated Medallion Quilts* (2012).

With much of my free-form work, I first decide on the basic form I'm going to use (such as Log Cabin, strippy, or medallion), then think about color and scale. Once I have worked out those general ideas, I just start in, building the parts and designing the quilt as I am constructing it. It's an exhilarating, adventuresome way to design because you stay involved and engaged throughout the entire project. When you work

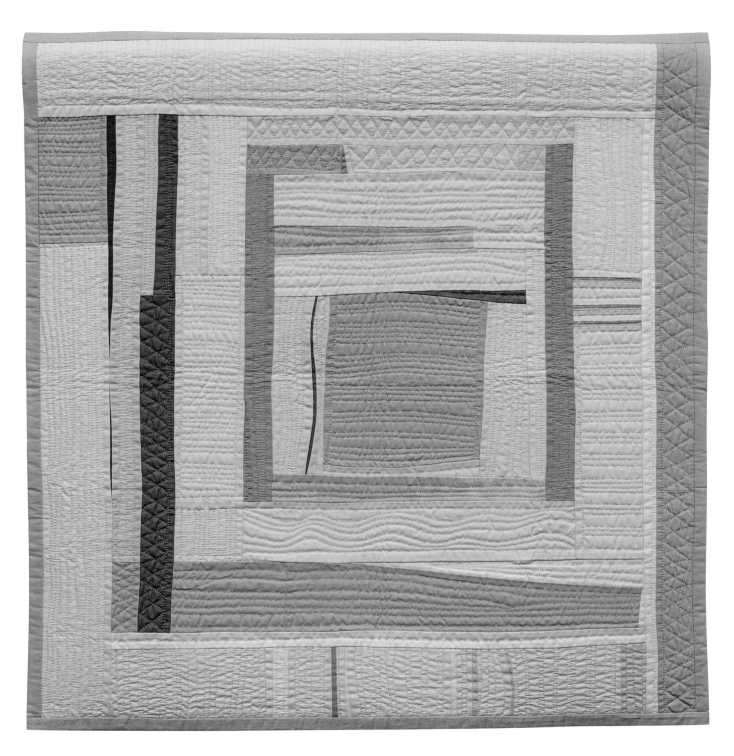

MEDALLION II, 33" × 33", 2010. Designed, made, and hand quilted by the author.

intuitively, you don't know what it's going to look like until it's finished, so excitement and expectation build as you work.

Working intuitively naturally produces surprising results because you haven't figured it all out in advance. That means as the work develops, you are likely to make adjustments, adding new colors or changing the scale of some of the sections. I think it becomes easier to see what is needed when a quilt is under construction rather than when it's just a plan on paper. It's a great way to work and it has been a big part of my education. I've found new ways to do things that work and I've found other ways that don't.

Another design process I use is to make rough pencil sketches of my ideas. I use them as a guide, like a map. I keep them in a sketchbook so I know where they are when I need them. I find this way of designing helpful when I'm making minimal, contemporary work, as with much of the work in this book.

In 2010, I developed another way to make sketches. Instead of pencil sketches, I make fabric sketches. I found that making sketches with the actual fabric I intended to use was a great way to work out composition and color. The first thirty-seven are shown in my book *37 Sketches*. Having added twenty since, I now have my own personal archive of artistic ideas, all numbered and readily accessible.

Because these Small Studies are completely developed and finished, they take on the added significance of small works of art. These sketches made up the featured exhibition at the Taupo Museum during the 2013 New Zealand Symposium. You can see some of them in this book shown with the larger quilts that grew from the initial Small Studies.

Do your homework. If you want to make minimal quilts or modern quilts, do some research. Today, many people use the Internet for this purpose and there is a tremendous amount of good information available just a click away. For a great treat, start with artist Mark Rothko, whom I mentioned in the introduction. But don't forget about the library—there's nothing like holding those books in your hands.

Have a conversation with your quilting friends, or artists who work in other mediums about how they design. Jean Wells, the many-faceted quilt artist, teacher, and author, uses photography and keeps journals to inspire her design work. She explains her methods in her two recent books by C&T Publishing: *Intuitive Color & Design: Adventures in Art Quilting* (2009); and *Journey to Inspired Art Quilting: More Intuitive Color & Design* (2012).

The one thing that is essential in the making of quilts, the one thing you absolutely have to have, is fabric. Here is how it works at my house. I have always liked working in solids. I use solids almost exclusively for work I classify as abstract art quilts because solids seem more painterly than prints, if for no other reason than paint comes in solids and never in prints. When I am designing new work, I don't know what I am going to need at the outset, so I want to have a good selection of solids on hand ready to use.

For example, the first thing I did when I started work on MEDALLION II (page 13) was to get out *every* light color I had, and I ended up using most of them in the quilt.

In my work I primarily use cottons, and mostly Kona cottons. They have been my mainstay because they have been around for a long time and have a great range of colors. You can get their color chart that's very helpful (especially if you live on a remote island). When working primarily with solids, consider adding some prints, or fabrics with texture like shot-cotton, linen, or raw silk.

Learn to trust your own ideas about designing. That was pretty much how quilts were designed in the eighteenth and nineteenth centuries, and there was some incredible work done in those years, mostly by women with no art degree. If they could do it, so can we. Be willing to take some risks. You are more likely to make a memorable quilt by taking some risks than by playing it too safe.

One more thing to remember is that the act of designing can sometimes be difficult. On certain days you can struggle and struggle and just not get anywhere. That happens to everyone, so don't feel defeated and as though it only happens to you. Judy Rantz is a friend of many years and a quiltmaker I admire. In a recent letter she talked about how she had been struggling with a project, but at last things were beginning to come together for her.

It is so exciting when inspiration and design competence occur at the same time. – Judy Rantz

Her comment made me laugh out loud. It's a very funny (but true) way to express the gratification we feel when design success comes after the initial and often inevitable struggle.

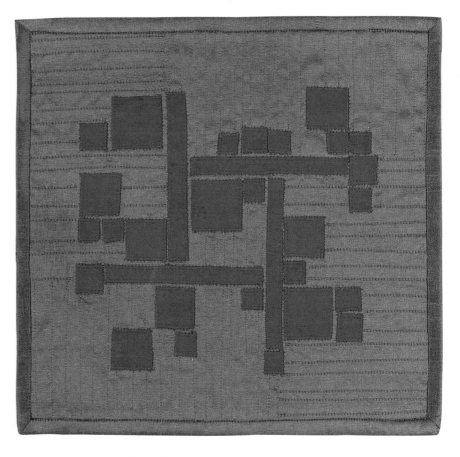

RED STUDY, 10" × 10½", 2013.
Made by Judy Rantz, Northport, Michigan.

Minimal Quilts

RED SQUARE IN PURPLE, 33" × 38", 2009. Designed, made, and hand quilted by the author.

so like beginning the first chapter of this book about minimal quilts with RED SQUARE IN PURPLE. While it's definitely minimal, its design roots are from the early 1800s. It is based on a New England quilt shown in Cyril Nelson's *The Quilt Engagement Calendar 1983: 2* (E.P. Dutton, 1982), Plate 4. (Remember reading about the very excellent calendars in the introduction?)

Discovering quilts like the c.1800 one is exactly why I'm always harping on the value of knowing what came before. The grandness of the old quilt, and others like it, is one of the reasons I value the tradition of quilting so much. There was an incredible number of extraordinarily well-designed quilts being made in the early days of our country. I've been trying, but it's hard to compete with what they were turning out. It's one of the reasons I have long treasured being associated with the unbroken line of quiltmakers. I like the idea of being a part of an art form that has most certainly been dominated by women.

I am not inclined to make quilts that express personal struggle, but SELF PORTRAIT (top right) was made during a period when I was feeling a bit off balance and un-centered. Expressing that feeling with my needle was a positive reaction and one that moved me in a constructive direction. Looking at it this many years later I do think it has a certain, dare I say minimal, panache to it.

MINIMAL I (right) is the kind of quilt I have a particular fondness for. It features minimal design, solid fabrics, and tight hand quilting that adds a soft organic texture to the work.

SELF PORTRAIT, 16½" x 21¼", 1989. Raw silk, designed, made, and hand quilted by the author.

MINIMAL I. 33" x 33", 2011. Designed, made, and hand quilted by the author. Private collection.

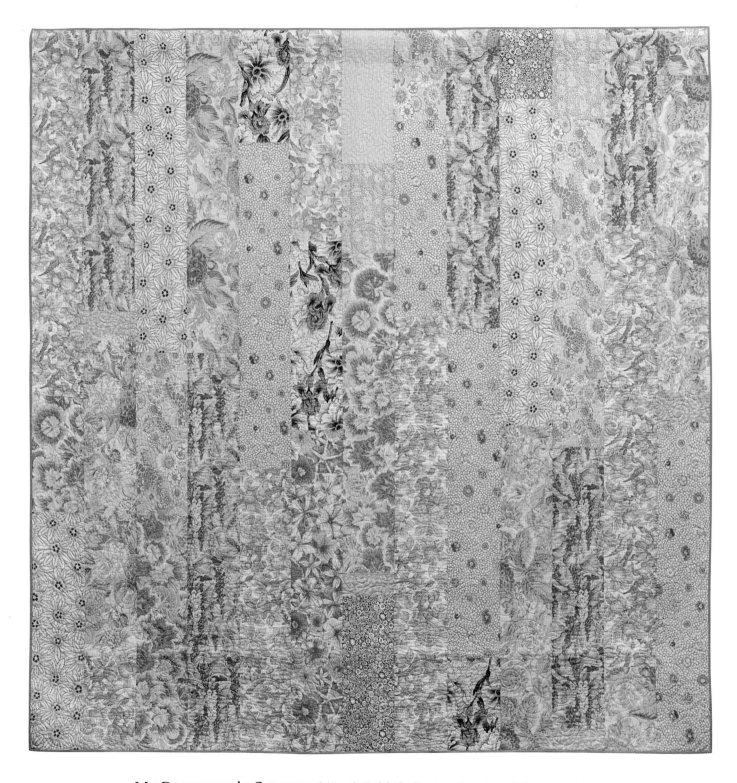

MY DAUGHTER'S GARDEN, 91" x 94", 2013. Designed and made by the author.
Machine quilted by Rogene Fischer, Manistee, Michigan.

My Daughter's Garden is a quilt I made for my daughter who perhaps loves gardening and is better at it than I am. As moms, we love it when our children actually do things better than we do. For us, it's a win-win situation, because we get to take the credit for their brilliance. My daughter is working and raising two active boys. She's busy. At the end of her long day, I wanted this quilt to be welcoming, quiet, and serene, but also a quilt she could enjoy and use without having to pamper it.

My goal was to make a truly beautiful quilt using stunning floral prints in light colors, so I set out to buy the fabric. Shopping for these delicious prints was as savory as choosing the flavor of your ice-cream cone at the best shop in town. I bought 12 half-yard pieces to round out what I had in my stash.

The idea was to make a simple bars quilt in light-colored floral prints with low contrast. As we all know, getting started is always the hardest part of just about anything. Therefore, I am going to "start" the instructions for making this quilt by telling you how I started.

To get an idea about fabric placement and how wide to make the bars, I made a visual with the fabric before I began cutting it. This is a matter of folding the fabric in the approximate width I think will work and arranging it by possible lengths and color. I laid it out on the floor—not the entire quilt by any means, but enough so I could evaluate what I envisioned before I started cutting the fabric.

What I'm talking about here is a really important concept in Liberated quilt construction. *You do not have to figure out everything before you start to sew.* You will make better decisions as you are in the process of constructing the quilt. This is because you can actually see how it is developing, right there in front of your eyes.

This is a pieced bars quilt, built on a simple concept of same-width and different-length strips, constructed with low-contrast fabrics. That seems to make it a contender for the Minimal quilt category.

This quilt looks deceptively easy to construct, and that sometimes lulls us into complacency. It is in this situation where I am most likely to let my guard down and live to regret it. What I found that helped me stay out of trouble when working on this quilt was just to pay attention to my basic sewing skills. These would include:

◆ Careful measuring (I think it's easier to do with a long measuring tape.)

◆ Careful and thorough pinning (I think silk pins work best, and pins should be no more than 4" apart.)

◆ Thorough pressing (I press to one side and press after each strip is added.)

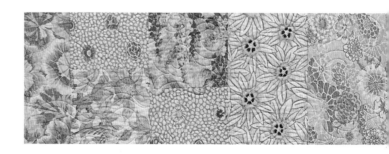

Bars Quilt How-To

1. Cut strips of a bunch of different prints 7½" x the width of the fabric.

2. Lay out three or four rows, changing the lengths and arranging the colors in a way that you like.

3. My rows were 94" loooooong. Oh, were they ever long! Hence, I would suggest careful pinning or you could easily have a wavy top that doesn't lie flat.

> **TIP:** I ended up making 13 rows and was glad I didn't sew them together until all 13 were pieced. Once I had the rows made, I moved them around more than once during the process of joining them all together. I also found joining (and pressing) them into groups of four made them easier to handle at the sewing machine.

My friend Marjorie Tucker is a young inventive quiltmaker and a popular quilt teacher. I admire her work and like to see how she has adapted Liberated techniques to make quilts in her own original style. Marge gives us a fine explanation of her first adventures in minimal construction and I'd say she figured it out on her own very successfully. Here is what she says about her three quilts, SPARK (page 21), SPLIT CHERRY (page 22), and FENCE (page 23).

When I got the request from Gwen to make a minimalist quilt for her new book, I was first thrilled to be asked. But then the panic set in! OK, it was not really panic, but a sense of "Huh? What is a minimalist quilt?"

Gwen provided her thoughts as well as a reference to minimalist artist Josef Albers. When I looked at his art, I realized that the use of color and line is very important in minimalist work, as well as the "distillation of the essence." You need to use the bare minimum to get your idea/point across. As Mies van der Rohe said, "Less is more."

I started sketching ideas the very night that I got Gwen's e-mail. My second sketch was SPARK (right). I got the idea to capture a flame or a match being struck. Using color and line, I tried to capture that moment. Quilting provided the texture of heat and light radiating out from the center. My mantra when making the sketches was "Keep it simple." It was difficult not to add stuff. In SPARK, I thought about cutting it in half horizontally, shifting the two halves, then rejoining. While this may have been interesting, it went against the mantra so I kept with the original plan.

SPLIT CHERRY (page 22) is an attempt to just work with line and color. Again, quilting was very important to provide texture as well as another layer of interest.

The idea for FENCE (page 23) came from an actual fence. My "quilty" eye was open

(continued on page 24)

SPARK, 36" x 54½", 2013. Designed, pieced, and machine quilted by
Marjorie Tucker, Boston, Massachusetts.

SPLIT CHERRY, 41½" × 49½", 2013. Designed, pieced, and machine quilted by
Marjorie Tucker, Boston, Massachusetts.

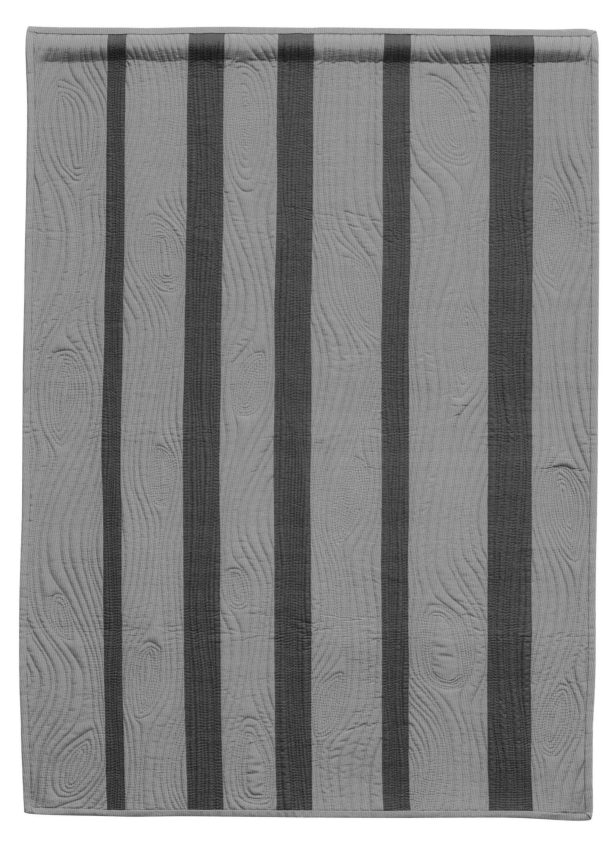

FENCE, 31" × 42½", 2013. Designed, pieced, and machine quilted by Marjorie Tucker, Boston, Massachusetts.

(from page 20)

that day as I drove past an old fence once painted barn red but now sun bleached to a terra cotta. The vertical lines and color drew me in. It was a simple idea, but not boring. I quilted curved lines designed to look like wood knots and wood grain (detail below).

I have really enjoyed working in this manner. As you can see, I made three quilts! Plus, it has given me a new way to approach quilt design. I have been inspired to continue to work in this vein with several more quilts sketched. Just the other day while driving I was struck by the pattern of light and shadow on a snow bank and quickly sketched that design when I got home. I can see myself continuing to incorporate minimalist design in my quilts. – Marjorie Tucker

Lynn Harris teaches quilting and writes about it in articles and on her blog (thelittlered hen.typepad.com). She has been making quilts long enough to be very good at it as you can see in ZINNIAS (page 25) and DAISY CHAIN (page 26). Here is what she says about her quilts.

We always plant a row of zinnias in our vegetable garden. When my daughter was younger, she enjoyed tending the zinnias while I weeded and harvested our vegetables. A photograph of our row of zinnias inspired me to make this quilt. In the photograph, the zinnias are in bright sun but the area behind them is in cool gray shadow. I tried to capture that feeling in this quilt. In keeping with the minimal look of the piecing and the organic inspiration for the design, the quilt is quilted with parallel wavy lines. I love that this quilt reminds me of time spent gardening with my daughter and to plant zinnias every year.

As for DAISY CHAIN (page 26), I saw this reverse-appliqué block in an antique red-and-white quilt. I wanted to try it but didn't want to make an entire quilt top of as many blocks as were in the antique version. My son challenged me to make quilts that didn't have a white background, so I chose some rich colors to try out the blocks. After making a few blocks I decided that I liked them in a chain, a daisy chain. This quilt takes me back to my younger days when I was first learning to sew; this particular shade of green and daisy chains were all the rage when I was in elementary school. DAISY CHAIN is quilted with parallel wavy lines that do not compete with the simplicity of the appliqué design. – Lynn Harris

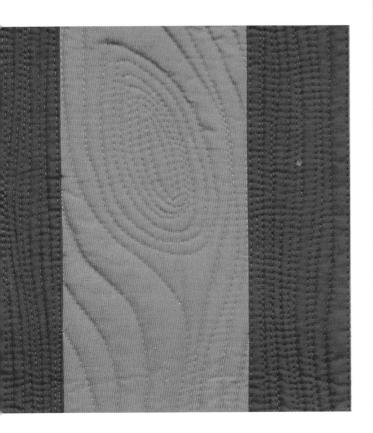

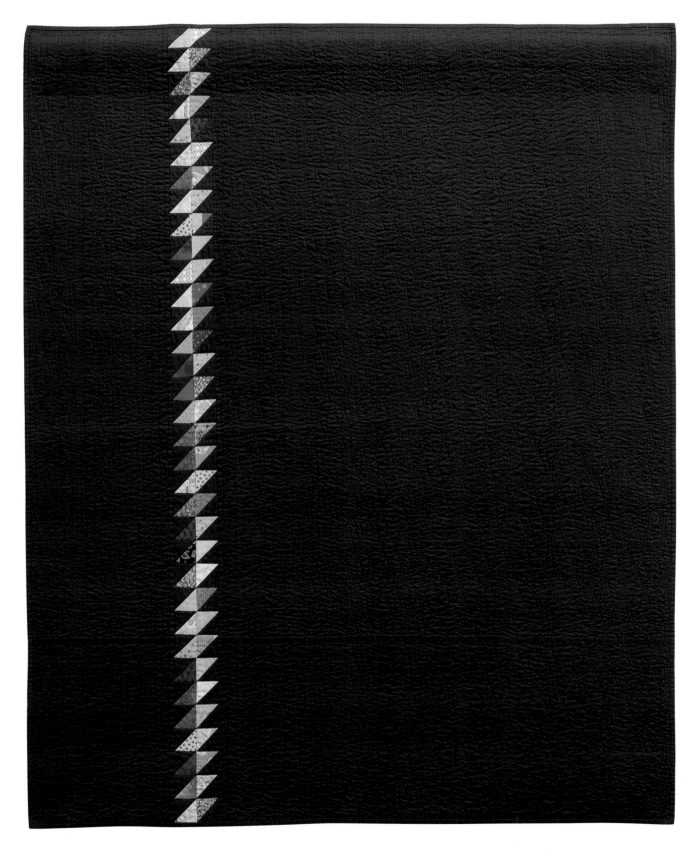

ZINNIAS, 44" × 52", 2011. Designed, made, and machine quilted by
Lynn Harris, Chelsea, Michigan.

DAISY CHAIN, 43" × 60", 2012. Designed, made, and machine quilted by
Lynn Harris, Chelsea, Michigan.

PASTELS WITH RED SQUARES (page 28) was designed in a different way, so let's talk about that. This quilt was made without a drawing and without actually measuring any of the parts.

I decided to try to work with some bright pastels so I just gathered some up, pulled ones I thought might work, and started folding them in different shapes and laying them out in an arrangement on the floor. Once I had a general idea of the sizes of the sections, I started building the major parts, deciding I'd work on the larger section on the right side first.

Here are the steps I used for making the larger right side:

◆ Cut the big yellow section.

◆ Cut the blue section below the big yellow part; sew a little yellow to one end and appliqué one red square. (The little yellow strip at the end of the blue strip will be adjacent to the large yellow piece when sewn together and it will create a new shape. This is a valuable trick you can add to your arsenal.)

◆ Sew a thin strip of red to the top of the orange piece.

◆ Join all three sections and the right side is finished. Press.

Next I began work on the left side:

◆ Cut the three long narrow pieces—the peach, blue, and yellow.

◆ Appliqué the red squares on the blue and add a strip of mustard at the base.

◆ Join those three pieces together. (You can see the yellow will again be adjacent to the larger yellow section on the right, which will create a new shape.) Press.

◆ Add a little strip of yellow at the top, again creating a new shape.

◆ With only the bottom section to make, lay the fabric in place, which will tell you about how big you need to cut the blue rectangle and purple outer strips. Oversize them a bit to be resized once constructed.

◆ Once this last part is together, lay it in position and see what it looks like. If it's way too big, you can decide which sides to trim, but still leave it a bit oversized just to make sure it will be big enough.*

◆ Stitch on the last piece. Press.

◆ Position the right and left sides together, pin thoroughly, sew them together, and press. Done!

* This is a good place to remind ourselves of the Liberated solution: If something is too short, add on. If something is too long, cut it off.

RED SQUARES ON WHITE LINEN (page 29) is another quilt featuring appliquéd squares, and it actually is the fifth quilt I've made in what is now a series of red-square quilts. Here's to the square!

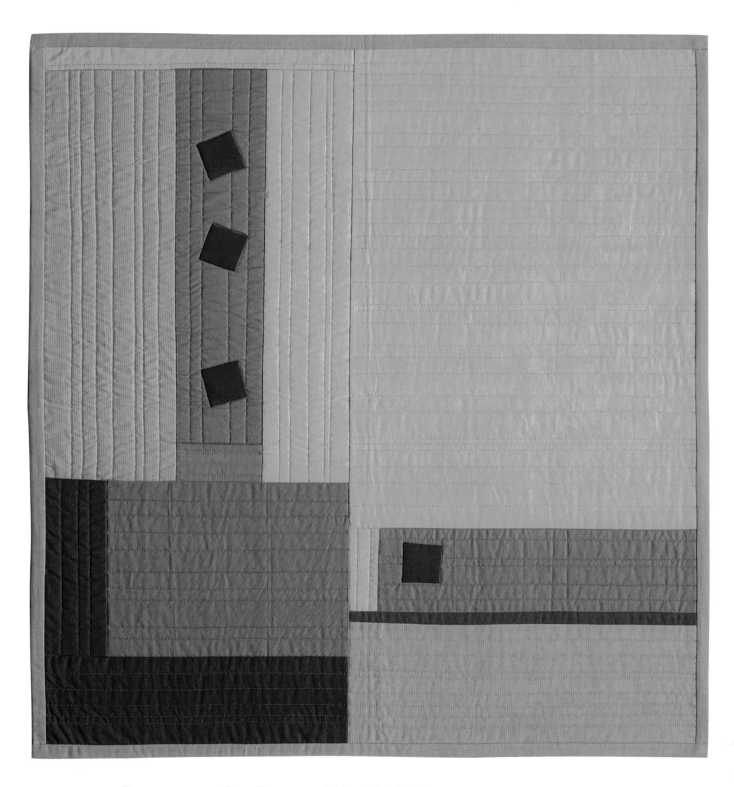

PASTELS WITH RED SQUARES, 31" x 32", 2013. Designed and made by the author.
Machine quilted by Rogene Fischer, Manistee, Michigan.

RED SQUARES ON WHITE LINEN, 29" x 34", 2012. Designed and made by the author.
Machine quilted by Rogene Fischer, Manistee, Michigan.

RED ON RED, 36" × 40", 2013. Designed and made by the author.
Machine quilted by Rogene Fischer, Manistee, Michigan.

TANGERINE, 32" x 32", 2013. Designed and made by the author.
Machine quilted by the team of Rogene Fischer and Gwen Marston.

The idea for RED ON RED (page 30) was to use different tones of the same color and large irregular shapes to produce a minimal effect. I tried to vary the tones enough to be effective, yet subtle enough as to not demand attention. Good lighting is everything when looking at this quilt.

TANGERINE (page 31 and detail below) pushes that idea further. It is so minimal, so very indistinct, that one must stand very close to it to discover the subdued tonal change. This quilt is an example of how the quilting stitches on a minimalist quilt are as essential as brush strokes on a minimalist painting. Their presence creates a subtle textural overlay.

The last three quilts shown in this chapter were made by Kathleen Glynn. I found Kathleen's pieces particularly intriguing and imaginative, partly because I don't think I've seen other work in any way similar to it. I was equally intrigued by her explanation about how she went about making them. Here is what Kathleen told me about her process.

I was inspired by your "minimal" idea and first set out to think about what "minimal" means to me.

I took some photos and noticed that just by changing the angle of my camera, I could find new lines for compositions. By looking at close-up photos from my garden (which is just a tidy term for "outdoors"), I started to see not petals but beautiful overlapping shapes. I made some small watercolor studies and exploded the scale of these organic compositions. Then, like a good Girl Scout, I looked at "real" artists like Ellsworth Kelly. I was always just a Google away from his work. I was definitely inspired by the colors he worked with and the narrowing down to simple primary colors.

Then I thought about exploding the scale of my shapes, yet minimizing lines. For instance, could I make a quilt with just two elegant and sexy stitching lines? Yep, I could.
– Kathleen Glynn

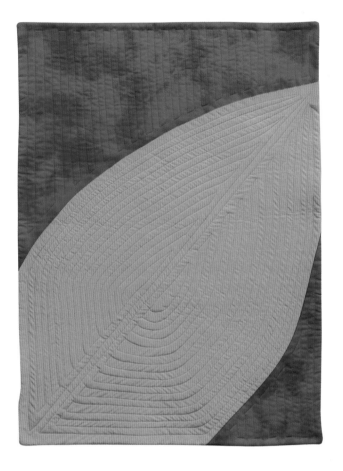

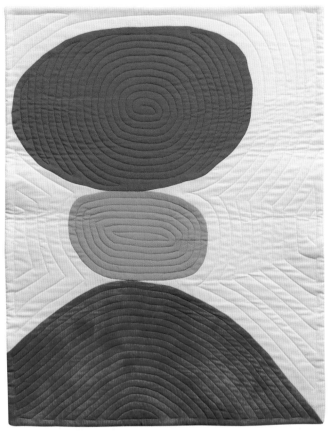

ABOVE: **LEAFY,** 23" × 29", 2013. Designed, pieced, and machine quilted by Kathleen Glynn, Central Lake, Michigan.

ABOVE RIGHT: **CAIRN,** 23" × 29", 2013. Designed, hand appliquéd, and machine quilted by Kathleen Glynn, Central Lake, Michigan.

RIGHT: **MOONTIME,** 23" × 29", 2013. Designed, pieced, and machine quilted by Kathleen Glynn, Central Lake, Michigan.

Hard-Edge Quilts

There is a style of minimal painting known as hard-edge painting that I'm very drawn to because it translates perfectly from paint to fabric. It's characterized by large, simplified geometric forms. The term "hard-edge painting" was coined in 1959 to describe the work of California painters who were painting "non-representative work with clear and sharp delineated areas of color." That automatically makes me think of quilts.

This style of hard-edge geometric abstraction began with earlier painters such as Wassily Kandinsky, Kazimir Malevich, and Piet Mondrian. The Russian painter Kandinsky (1866–1944) deserves special mention as he is considered one of the most important innovators in modern art and is often called the "Father of Abstract Art." Other well-known modern artists associated with hard-edge painting are Frank Stella, Kenneth Noland, Josef Albers, and Ellsworth Kelly.

The definition of hard-edge painting seems to apply to many quilts that I've made adhering to those classical characteristics. It's worth mentioning that in today's art quilt movement, a current trend encourages cutting fabric without rulers. The resulting work is less quilt-like and therefore, some think, more art-like. My view is that cutting with or without rulers isn't the defining factor of whether something is or isn't art. Certainly, both methods of cutting can produce artful quilts. I do like the look of curved lines and use them in my quilts too, as seen in MEDALLION II (page 49). But at the same time, I also remain committed to the school of hard-edged art and hard-edged quilts.

Quilts in this category appear deceptively simple. They are the kind of work that has historically triggered the response, "My five-year-old could make that." What I have found when working in this style is that they are some of the more challenging quilts I've made. When there is less, everything counts more. And when you are working in solid fabrics, line delineation is sharp and clear—you see *everything* and, therefore, everything matters more. I will also say that I am completely captivated by this style of quilt and will definitely continue working in this style.

Having confessed that these quilts are not easy to make, I just now have discovered that they are also not easy to write about. Except for the last two quilts, TURQUOISE (page 47) and ORANGE ON WHITE (page 48), designing them

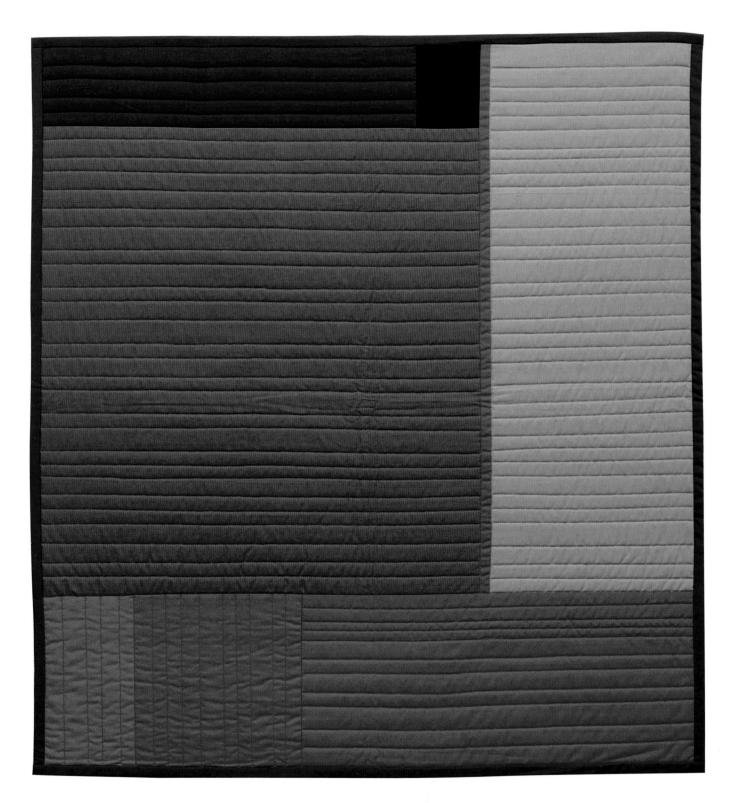

MINIMAL IN LAVENDER, RED, AND GREEN, 36" × 39", 2013.
Designed and made by the author. Machine quilted by Rogene Fischer, Manistee, Michigan.

MINIMAL COMPOSITION, 32" x 32", 2011. Designed, made, and hand quilted by the author.

involved thinking of ways to divide up the space in a different and interesting way.

I most often begin by making a series of rough sketches. I draw squares and/or rectangles and divide up the space by drawing lines this way and that until I get one that shows possibility. I use the drawing as a map, not a blueprint. In other words, the map helps me see where I'm going, but it doesn't restrict me from taking a side road if it occurs to me. It's a guide, but it allows me to make changes as the work develops.

Once I have a rough sketch that I like, the next step is to select some colors I think might work. "Might" is the operative word here. Eventually some get taken away and others are added. Once you begin to build the quilt, it becomes easier to make color decisions. The key to working this way is that while you have a rough plan and you have a group of colors chosen, you are not bound by either the plan or the colors. You inevitably make better choices, because as you watch the work develop, you can see the actual piece!

When you see it right in front of you, it is much easier to make good choices than if you were just to follow your initial plan "verbatim." Another advantage to working this way is that the time spent planning is much greater because the planning continues throughout the entire construction of the work. You don't spend an hour or two planning the quilt; rather your mind is actively involved, consciously and subconsciously, evaluating the work as it grows, and it doesn't stop until the binding is on.

These quilts consist of big color fields. They rely on the quilting stitches to create texture and also a secondary design. The difference in the look of them before and after quilting is dramatic. Without the quilting, they sometimes seem a little scary to me. I have to just keep the faith and go to work figuring out the best way to quilt them. Because the quilting is such an integral part of this type of quilt, you have to take it seriously, whether it's by hand or machine.

In my quilt MINIMAL COMPOSITION (left and detail below), I used groups of straight-line hand quilting to add texture. MINIMAL II (page 38) also has straight-line quilting, but done by machine. When it came time to quilt the even more minimal pieces, MINIMAL COMPOSITION IN PURPLE AND GREEN (page 39) and MINIMAL III (page 40), I used this same idea with closely quilted straight lines going in different directions with variations in the spacing. I like the look of close-line quilting because it's reminiscent of the way our Pakistani and Indian sisters have traditionally quilted their quilts. While these two were machine quilted, I use the same idea in some of the hand-quilted work that I do.

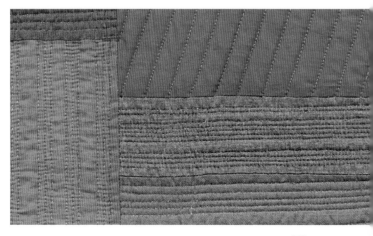

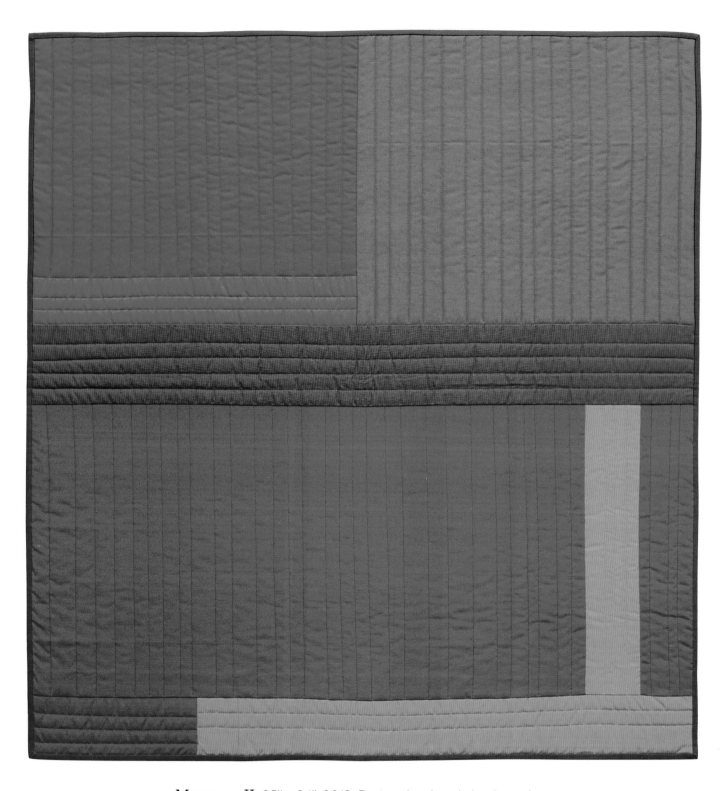

MINIMAL II, 35" x 36", 2013. Designed and made by the author.
Machine quilted by Rogene Fischer, Manistee, Michigan.

MINIMAL COMPOSITION IN PURPLE AND GREEN, 33" x 33", 2012. Designed and made by the author. Machine quilted by the team of Rogene Fischer and Gwen Marston.

MINIMAL III, 30" × 32", 2013. Designed and made by the author.
Machine quilted by the team of Rogene Fischer and Gwen Marston.

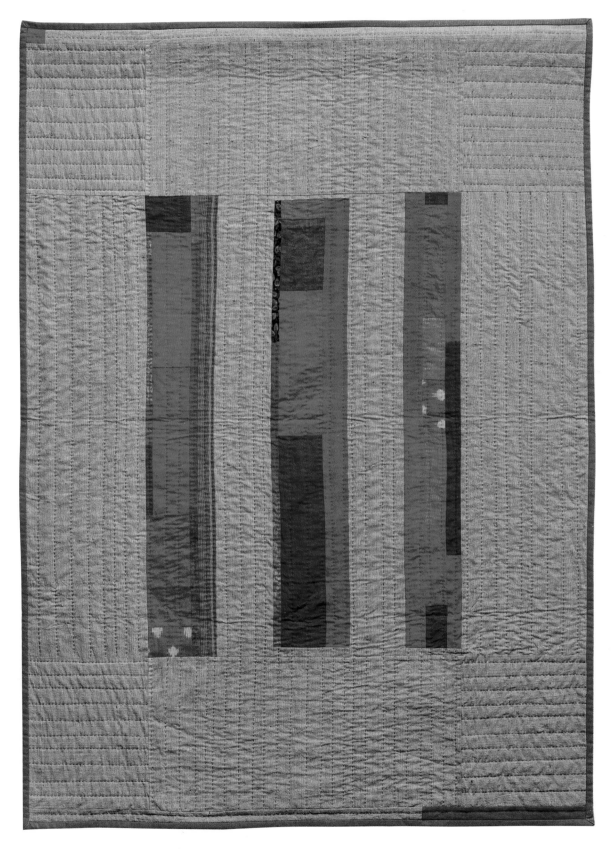

THREE BARS, 48" x 65", 2013. Designed, made, and hand quilted by
Joanne Salz, San Rafael, California.

Joanne Salz looked to traditional Amish quilts as the inspiration for her quilt THREE BARS (page 41). Here is Joanne talking about her quilt.

> When I think of minimal quilts, I think of Amish Quilts. (Gwen, your Amish Quilting Designs book is showing me other ways to think!) I kept working on the design to distill it down to the simplest form—just the three red bars on a neutral background. Since the neutral has a directional weave, if you look closely there are squares in the corners facing another direction to give a tiny hint of an Amish corner. Then, of course, since I'm me, I had to put several reds in the bars, then a bit on the ends, then quilt it in both red linen and hand-dyed cotton threads. – Joanne Salz

Kristin Shields is an Oregon quiltmaker and teacher who has been making Liberated quilts for a long time. (She blogs at *kristinshields. typepad.com*.) I think she has a special affinity for design and for putting color together as you can see in her quilt MINIMAL PURPLE (far right and detail right) and IRIS DREAMS (page 44). Kristin made IRIS DREAMS for her Modern Quilt Guild Challenge in 2012.

As an experienced quilter she has well-thought-out ideas about the quilts she makes. In MINIMAL PURPLE she used a combination of [...] nd hand quilting. I asked her about [...] e is what she said.

> I like to combine hand and machine quilting because I often don't have time to hand quilt a whole quilt, but I do have time to add some hand stitching in certain areas. The hand stitching serves to highlight the focus areas and draws the eye in. I also use it to add pops of color that are more subtle than a machine-stitched line would be. – Kristin Shields

You can see how effective this is by looking at the close-up of Kristin's quilt.

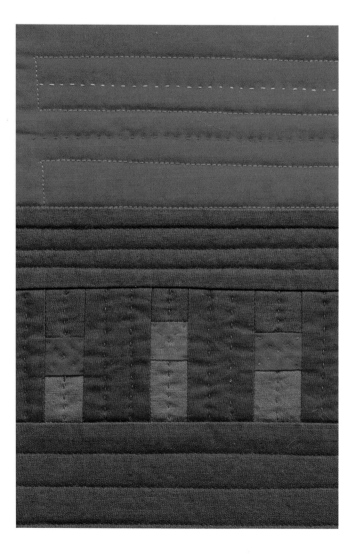

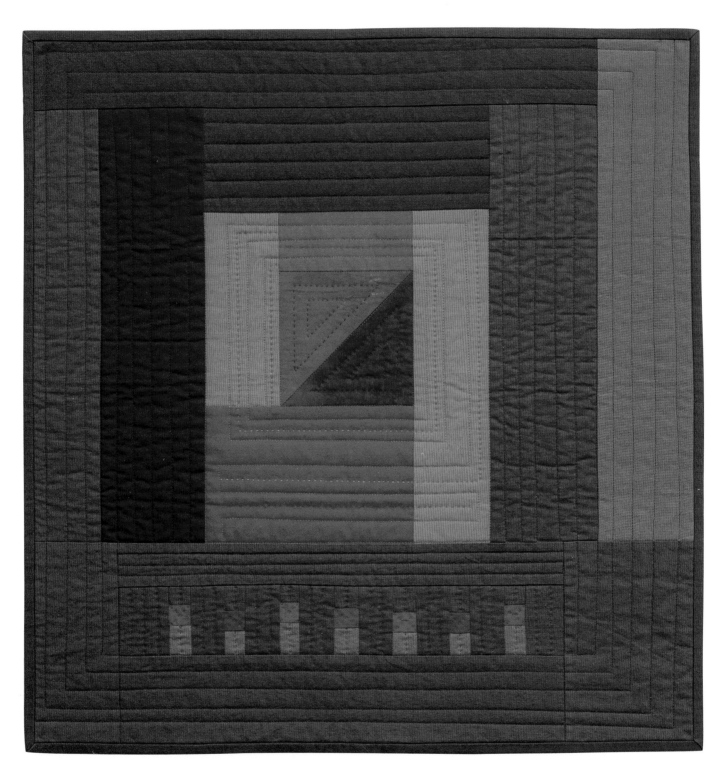

MINIMAL PURPLE, 25" × 26", 2012. Designed, made, and
hand and machine quilted by Kristin Shields, Bend, Oregon.

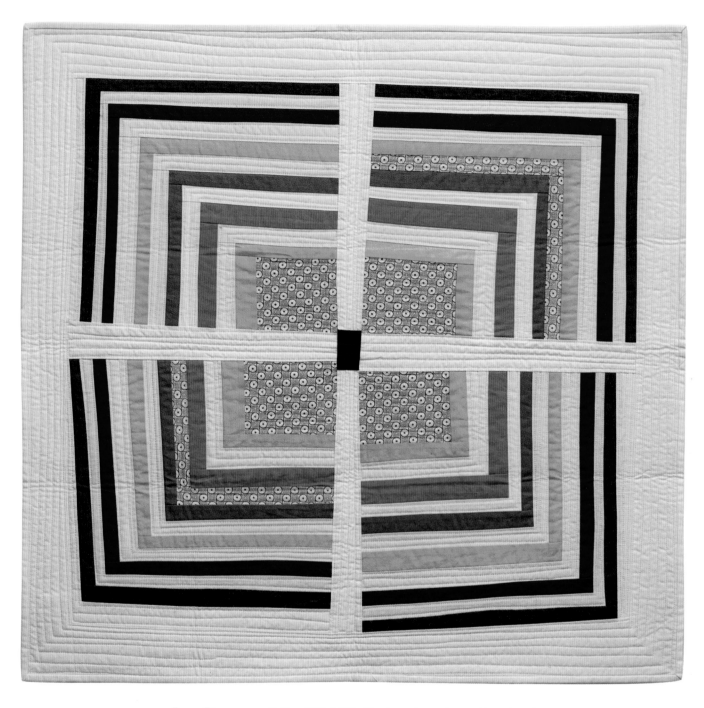

IRIS DREAMS, 34" × 32", 2012. Designed, made, and hand and machine quilted by Kristin Shields, Bend, Oregon.

Here are Kristin's views about working in a minimal style.

When I thought about these quilts, I considered architecture, man-made items, and minimal landscapes. I also thought about symmetry and balance. I noticed in Josef Albers's work that his paintings are often very symmetrical. Many times they do not follow the Rule of Thirds, which is something I consider quite a lot. However, the minimal modern quilts are often deliberately asymmetrical—just something I was thinking about yesterday. I think I could get a lot of ideas by taking photos of buildings around town. – Kristin Shields

Kristin's mention of the Rule of Thirds puzzled me because I did not know what it was. She explained that it is a photographic concept that involves dividing a composition into thirds—top to bottom and left to right— and using the intersection points to create an asymmetrical composition. Kristin says when creating asymmetrical work she often uses this concept, although she did not use it in her two quilts shown here.

MINIMAL STUDY #1 (below) was made by Carol Van Sickle, who is one of those needlewomen who have spent their lives honing both their technical and design skills to the point where they are successful in whatever they create. Carol can construct very complicated, detailed work, but can also do simple but well-designed pieces.

MINIMAL STUDY #1, 16¾" × 21", 2013. Designed, made, and stitched in the ditch by Carol Van Sickle, Prudenville, Michigan.

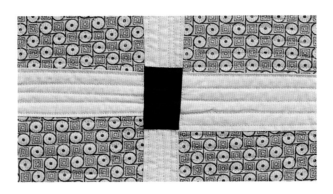

Nancy Perkins has come to my quilt retreats over the years and I've always admired her work. I'm pleased to be able to share two of her recent quilts, which I found utterly refreshing.

Here is what Nancy said about her color studies (this page).

I am totally intrigued by Gwen's fabulous Small Studies series of quilts. The minimal, contemporary quilt style is catching my attention more and more. This quilt is my attempt at combining the two.

As a primarily primitive quilter, I have recently become more and more interested in the look of the new contemporary, minimal quilts. I decided to start small in my first attempts at this new style for me, as you can see in these two quilts. – Nancy Perkins

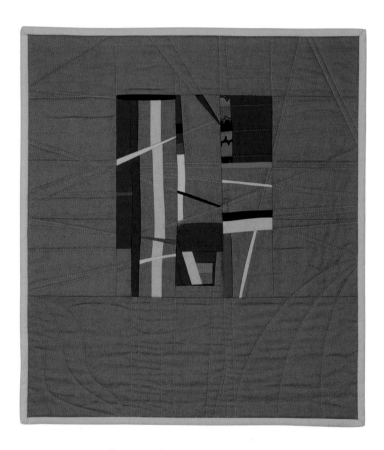

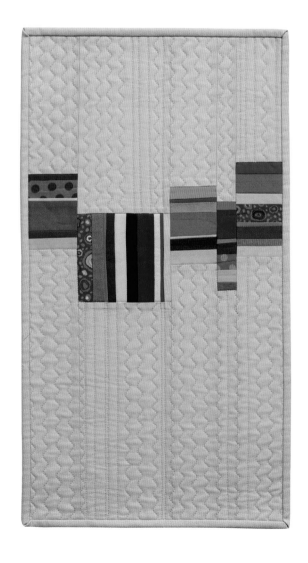

ABOVE: COLOR STUDY #29, 16½" × 18½", 2013. Designed and made by Nancy Perkins, Suwanee, Georgia. Machine quilted by Nancy Poorbaugh of Finally Finished, Montgomery, Alabama.

RIGHT: COLOR STUDY #30, 12½" × 22½", 2013. Designed and made by Nancy Perkins, Suwanee, Georgia. Machine quilted by Nancy Poorbaugh of Finally Finished, Montgomery, Alabama.

TURQUOISE began with the idea of making a pieced back. I wasn't long into making it when I changed my mind and liked what was developing so much, I saw it as a piece that could stand on its own. This is not the first time that I have made a back that I felt was worthy and sometimes wondered if the back rivaled the front and may have categorically been the better side of the quilt.

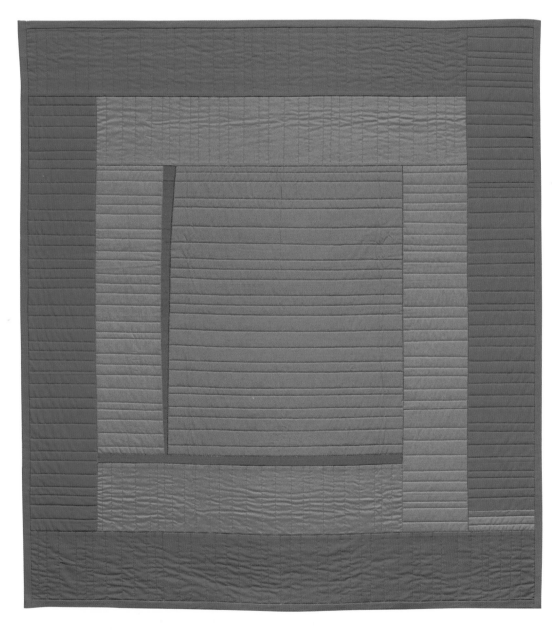

TURQUOISE, 41" x 45", 2013. Designed and made by the author.
Machine quilted by Rogene Fischer, Manistee, Michigan.

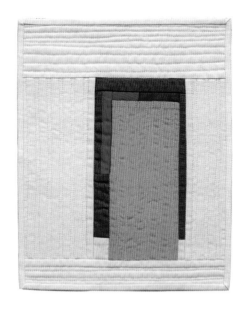

Once in a while I'm given a fresh new design by the Quilt Fairy for no other reason than maybe that I've been exceptionally good. One day when I was busy experimenting with new minimal quilt designs, the idea for ORANGE ON WHITE (below) was magically lying right there on my cutting table: a little orange rectangle on top of a bit of purple just barely showing, and both on top of a larger piece of white. It created the effect of the orange hanging down into the white. What a good idea. I set about sewing these scraps together into SMALL STUDY # 57 (left).

Exploring possibilities by making a small study is one of the new methods I have found useful in testing out a design idea before I invest time and money in making a larger piece.

ABOVE: SMALL STUDY #57,
9" × 11", 2013.
Designed, made, and machine
quilted by the author.

RIGHT: ORANGE ON WHITE,
34" × 43", 2013.
Designed and made by
the author.
Machine quilted by
Rogene Fischer
Manistee, Michigan.

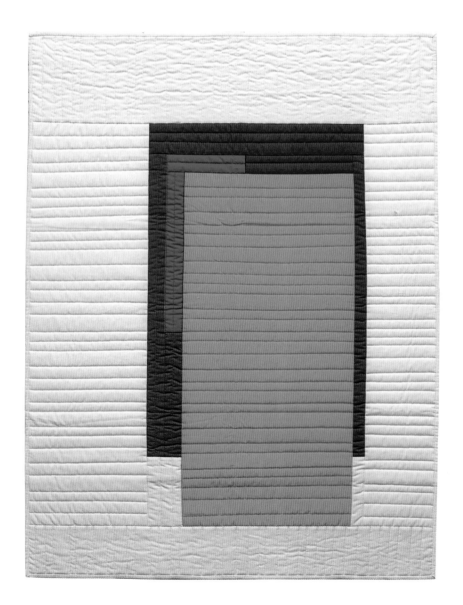

Minimal Color

MEDALLION II, 33" × 33". Designed, made, and hand quilted by the author.

r

hinking about what exactly
minimal," I wondered if
ay the color would make it
unal. Certainly quilts without high
ot would appear less busy, and "less"
part of what makes something minimal. It
also seemed that I might be able to enhance
the minimal look by using uncomplicated
design, something that could be immediately
understood without an enormous amount of
intellectual effort. The quilts in this chapter
show my attempt to make minimal quilts using
the idea of less color and less design.

For someone who for years has felt most
comfortable using strong, saturated colors,
I surprised myself by how much I enjoyed
working with neutrals. For a moment, I actually
began to wonder if I might never return to
strong colors again.

I do think that the neutrals give these quilts
a sense of lightness. With so little color and
barely any contrast, they are almost transparent.
They certainly are less noticeable. When you
walk into the room, they don't demand your
instant attention. They are quiet, serene, and
restful. If you put them on the bed, you can
count on them to stay there. When dressed in
neutrals as they are, words like "sophisticated"
and "understated" are fitting. Recognizing
the power of color, these same quilts worked
in bold color might not appear minimal, and
descriptive words like "bold" or "robust" would
come to mind.

TIP: I found that when limiting myself to
neutrals, having a good collection of them
was very helpful. Introducing even slight
variations added subtle changes that made
the works more interesting. I used a Kona
color chart as a reference in selecting a wide
variety of light tones.

MEDALLION II (page 49) is one of the first
quilts I made using just neutrals. This quilt is
one in a series of quilts I made with the idea
of constructing three quilts using the same
ideas—a minimal medallion format using large,
simple shapes, and only very slight changes to
create three individual pieces.

Some of the traditional formats for putting
a quilt together have been broadly known and
practiced. For example, a strippy quilt is made of
odd-sized pieces of fabrics and sewn together in
rows. It doesn't require a pattern, you can make
it out of available scraps, it invites innovation,
and everyone can do it—all of which add to
its popularity. An added bonus is that most
strippy quilts are visually interesting and often
artistically successful.

Here is the story of how I made my STRIPPY
quilt (right). I started making the rows, moved
them around, and began piecing narrow strips
to go between the rows. As I added onto the
rows, I tried to keep my eye on how the fabrics
were interacting with their neighbors. Since the
goal was to keep it minimal, I reminded myself
to keep it simple while still making it interesting
in a soft, understated way.

STRIPPY, 45" x 56", 2012. Designed and made by the author.
Machine quilted by Rogene Fischer, Manistee, Michigan.

MINIMAL IN NEUTRALS, 35" × 35", 2012. Designed, made, and hand quilted by the author.

At first, when I didn't have very much sewn together, it looked boring; but as other parts went up, I could see that it was beginning to take shape. And that is always the way it works when you are making quilts in the Liberated way. You have to get started, add a little something, and keep going. This is an important concept to get your head around. Once you have a few Liberated quilts under your belt, you will gain confidence in yourself and the process.

One of the things I like so much about the Liberated process—about working without patterns, about figuring it out as it's being made—is that you stay completely engaged from beginning to end. And at the end you have a quilt you not only made, but that you also designed. That's rewarding. That's affirming.

You will find that as you work on building the rows, the more you get put together, the easier it becomes to see what is needed and when enough is enough. What I find so rewarding about making a quilt like this is that while I'm very much making a quilt that comes *directly* from "the tradition of quiltmaking," it also has a decidedly contemporary look. It is definitely a great choice for someone who appreciates the tradition but also wants to do original work. No pattern needed here. Rather, it is a matter for each of us to get started and use our own ideas as we make our own original strippy quilt.

> **TIP:** If you want to make your strippy quilt bigger, make more rows and make them longer.

MINIMAL IN NEUTRALS (left) is made with cottons, but the large white area is fine linen. This quilt was a three-part design process starting with a rough pencil sketch, followed by my SMALL STUDY #53 (below), and finally the construction of the quilt. The advantage of making the small study was that I completely worked out the composition, color, and construction issues, using it in the same way that a painter uses a sketch. I have found making these small studies to be an enjoyable and very effective way to work out color and composition. With this quilt, I was definitely trying to pare it down to its essentials—simple design, limited colors.

SMALL STUDY #53, 9½" × 11½", 2012. Designed and made by the author. This quilt was my "sketch" for MINIMAL IN NEUTRALS (left).

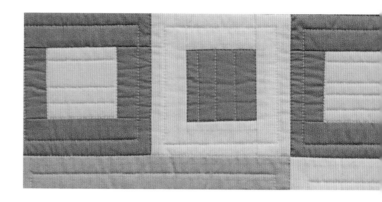

This quilt clearly shows how you can create new shapes by adjacent color placement. By piecing in a small white rectangle in the adjacent darker section on the left, the white shape is visually changed. On the right side, the pink border takes a jog to the left near the top of the quilt. Learning how to use this in your work is a clever way to add an unexpected element, which can add new dimensions to the piece.

To credit this clever idea, I learned about it from seeing it on antique quilts, and noticed what a nice effect it was. You will see it in a lot of my work. I used it in the very first LIBERATED STAR quilt I made back in 1991, shown in *Liberated Quiltmaking* (AQS, 1996, page 134). Further discussion about adjacent color placement is covered in chapter 19 of that same book. Look at the antique LONE STAR quilt (page 176) and you will see other ways to use adjacent color placement. Sometimes it's very obvious, and other times just a subtle shift.

FRAMED SQUARES (far right and detail above) is built on a simple idea: the same block in two different sizes with slight variations and a limited number of neutrals. The layout of the blocks is orderly and symmetrical. There are no unexpected surprises.

When my friend Pam Beal saw this quilt she said, "Isn't it interesting what can be done with pale color and one or two ideas. Playing with the scale of the blocks really gives movement, doesn't it?" And she's exactly right. I was trying to make a quiet minimal quilt, and was surprised at how much movement those little blocks created as a result of being smaller and ever so slightly more colorful.

I think Rogene Fisher's straight-line quilting is just right for this quilt. There is enough quilting, but not too much. The quilt is not stiff as can happen when heavily machine quilted and I like that. The straight lines have some variation, but you have to look for it. I think it's very good.

The instructions for this quilt begin on page 64.

The majority of minimal art is abstract work, but there is representative work as well. I consider the WINTER BEECH (page 56) to fit that category. Winter in the north country, which is right outside my windows, inspired this quilt. The woods close to my house are full of mature maples and beech. I'm not a poet, but looking at these elegant trees, bare of their leaves and standing straight and tall in the snowy woods, prompted this short verse.

Beech, with its smooth gray skin
in winter shows its bones.

Gwen Marston

FRAMED SQUARES, 60" x 60", 2012. Designed and made by the author.
Machine quilted by Rogene Fischer, Manistee, Michigan.

WINTER BEECH, 18" × 20", 2012. Designed, made, and hand quilted by the author.

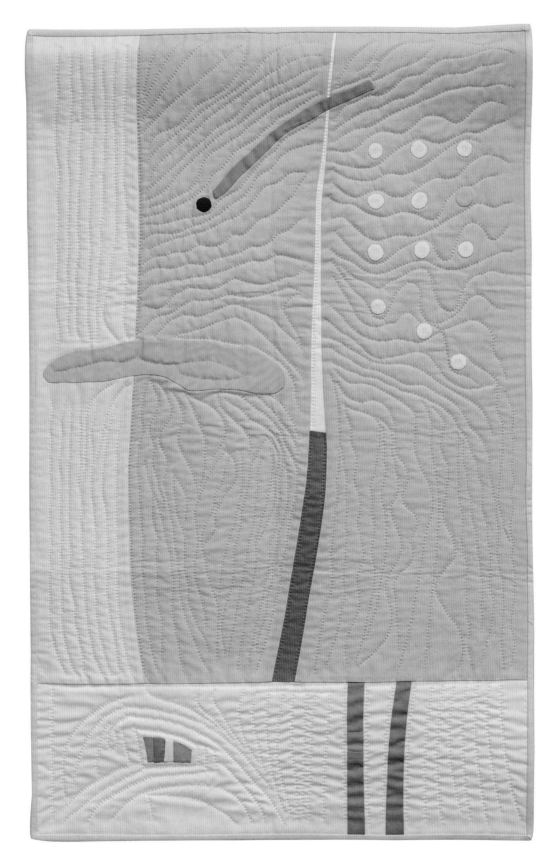

LILY PAD Á LA MODE, 24" × 38½", 2013. Designed, made, and hand quilted in a floor frame by Pam J. Beal, Mass City, Michigan.

Lily Pad á la Mode (page 57) was made by Pam Beal, who lives in the Upper Peninsula in Michigan that gets a lot more winter snow than I do here on Beaver Island. You have to be independent and determined to live up there, and Pam does it with ease. She brings this same independent spirit to her quilting, as you can see in her work. Here is what she says about this quilt.

When presented with an abstract design, the imagination gets busy. The name of this quilt is a reflection of what two people—my husband, Wayne, and I—saw in this quilt. The quilted line is an improvisation playing with the forms and lines of the composition.
– Pam Beal

Kuba Composition (right), made by Cathy Jones, was inspired by the colors and shapes borrowed from traditional early-twentieth-century hand-woven and appliquéd raffia dance skirts from Zaire. She used natural-dyed fabrics to get the earthy, soft colors and created quite a showstopper. This quilt is hand appliquéd and hand quilted by Cathy, who lives on Beaver Island. She is a very accomplished quilter, and it's nice to have her just around the corner to discuss the finer points of quilting when they need to be discussed. She also knits and knows all about baking bread, which makes her competent in all things that truly matter.

Jan Tetzlaff used neutrals to make Santa Barbara (left). Jan has learned one of the most important skills that artists need to acquire—the act of careful observation. We can find inspiration for our work all around us. If we practice "looking" we can learn how to "see."

Here is what Jan says about her quilt.

This quilt was inspired by tile work that mimicked the waves that I saw during a visit to the California beach town of Santa Barbara. I used a variety of linens and woven fabrics accented by hand stitching to add texture. – Jan Tetzlaff

LEFT: Santa Barbara, 24" x 26", 2013. Designed, made, and hand quilted by Jan Tetzlaff, Bend, Oregon.

KUBA COMPOSITION, 41½" × 51½", 2013. Designed, made, and hand quilted by
Cathy Jones, Beaver Island, Michigan.

Carol Van Sickle is another multitalented needlewoman. I've known her for thirty years, during which time she's been busy making beautiful quilts and winning her share of prizes, especially for her impeccable hand quilting. Besides quilting, she does bobbin lace, crochets, knits socks by the dozens, and lately has been knitting fine lace shawls with incredibly complex patterns. She grew up with an artist for a dad, and rather naturally developed a good eye for design as you can see in her NEUTRAL STUDY #1 and NEUTRAL STUDY #2 (this page).

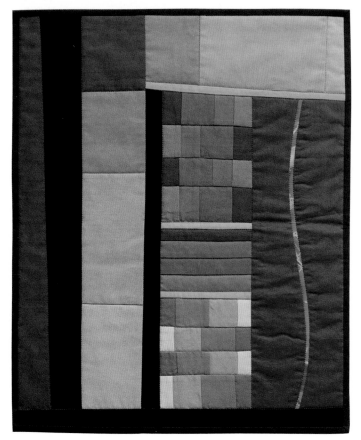

TOP LEFT: NEUTRAL STUDY #1,
20½" × 23½", 2013.
Designed, made, and stitched
in the ditch by Carol Van Sickle,
Prudenville, Michigan.

LEFT: NEUTRAL STUDY #2,
15¼" × 19¼", 2013.
Designed, made, and stitched
in the ditch by Carol Van Sickle,
Prudenville, Michigan.

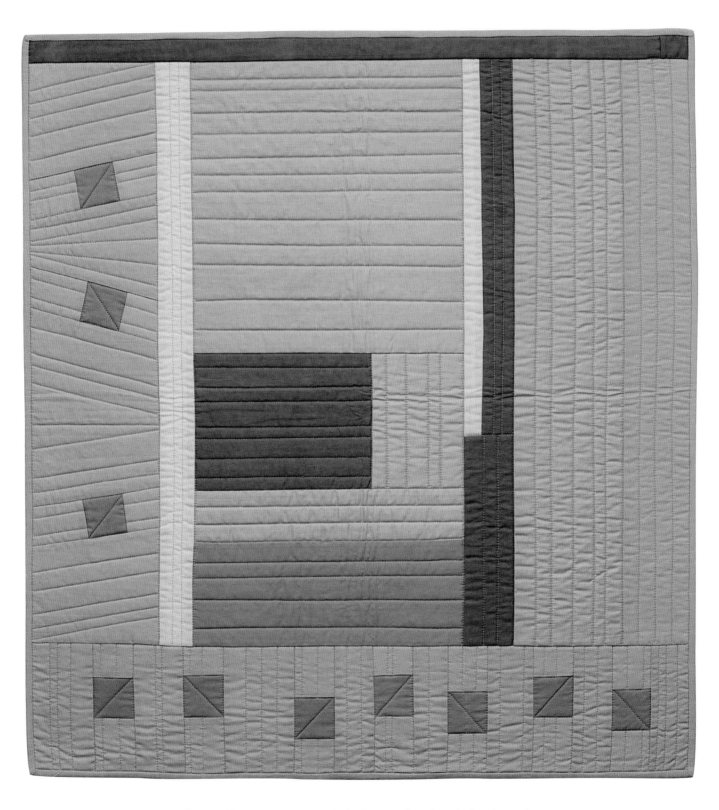

SPLIT PEA, 30" × 32", 2013. Designed and made by the author.
Machine quilted by Rogene Fischer, Manistee, Michigan.

In the Minimal Quilts chapter there are two quilts that sport appliquéd squares (Pastels with Red Squares, page 28, and Red Squares on White Linen, page 29). Split Pea (page 61) has squares that are pieced into the two borders: three angled squares along one side (detail left) and a bunch of squares jumping up and down on the bottom border. I confess to being enamored with my relatively new idea of adding miscellaneous squares to my quilts. When I find something new that I like, it has been known to become my default solution to every design question.

Adding squares is another way you can add interest to your quilt, and it's not at all difficult—two reasons that made me want to use them on every quilt once I figured it out. You can set squares in straight and line them up in a row, or set them straight but vary the heights, or set them on an angle.

Setting-in Squares How-To

Before you read these instructions, take a look at figures 1–3, which illustrate what you will be making and how you will set the squares into the border. Figure 1 shows the strip-set that will be cut into individual units and inserted into the border. Figure 2 shows that the sidepieces on either side of the squares need to be long enough to accommodate the various placements when inserted into the border. Figure 3 shows how the units are inserted on an angle.

Instead of making each unit separately, it's quicker to make a strip-set and cut each unit the size as indicated by the dotted lines in figure 1. Here is how that is done.

◆ Determine how big you want the finished squares to be, how many you want, and how you want them arranged. One good way to do this is to make a visual; cut actual finished size squares and position them on the border. That way, you can see exactly what it will look like and it will give you an idea about how many units you will need to make. This exercise is a test case. You don't have to do it for all four sides; just cut enough squares to give yourself a clearer idea about what size and approximately how many squares you may want to start with.

◆ Once you know the size of the finished squares, cut a strip of fabric that width plus ½" for seam allowance.

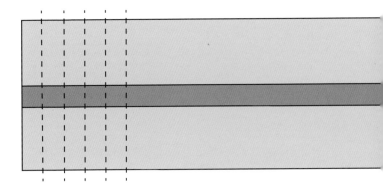

Fig. 1

◆ Look at figure 2 and notice that the sidepiece on either side of the square (which is the border fabric) needs to be longer than the width of the border. The objective is to make the sidepieces long enough so that you either line them up straight, piece them in on an angle, or make them move up and down. If you plan to place them at an angle or move them up and down, you need the units to be a little longer to accommodate that.

◆ Piece the strip-set as shown in figure 1 and press. Whatever width you cut the center strip is the size you now will cut the individual units from the strip-set (figure 1).

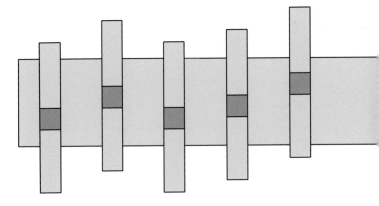

Fig. 2

◆ Figure 2 shows how the squares are set in at different heights.

◆ Figure 3 shows how the squares are set in on an angle. Cut the angles, sew the unit on one side of the border, and press it. Use your ruler and rotary cutter to trim off the extra fabric even with the border. Sew on the other side of the border.

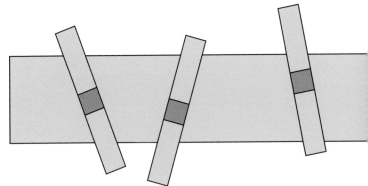

Fig. 3

◆ Once you have added the squares, press the border strip, measure and cut it to the length of your border, and it's ready to add to your quilt.

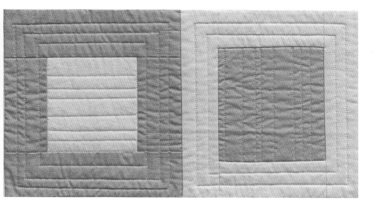

Take a look at FRAMED SQUARES (page 55) and you will notice that I use a slight variation of the lightest tones and the darker gray tones. Working at limiting the colors, I used three tones of gray—a cream, off-white, and ice pink. There are also two slight variations of the larger 10" blocks—15 with smaller white centers framed in gray and 14 with large gray centers framed in white.

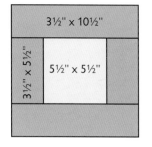

FIG. 1. Make 15.

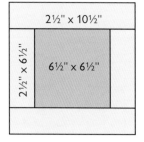

FIG. 2. Make 14.

FIG. 3. Make 14.

FIG. 4. Make 14.

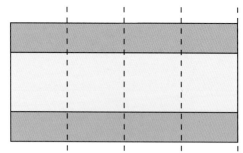

FIG. 5

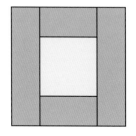

FIG. 6

FRAMED SQUARES HOW-TO

This quilt has 29 large blocks and 28 small blocks.

Making the Large Blocks

There are two size variations of the larger 10" x 10" (finished) blocks: 15 blocks with smaller white centers framed in gray and 14 blocks with large gray centers framed in white.

◆ Make 15 blocks with smaller white centers framed in gray (figure 1).
  ◆ Cut 15 – 5½" x 5½" white squares.
  ◆ Cut 30 – 3" x 5½" gray strips
  ◆ Cut 30 – 3" x 10½" gray strips.

◆ Sew the 5½" strips to opposite sides of the square and press. Add the 10½" strips to the remaining two sides. Press. *

◆ Make 14 blocks with the larger gray centers framed in white (figure 2).
  ◆ Cut 14 – 6½" x 6½" gray squares.
  ◆ Cut 28 – 2½" x 6½" white strips
  ◆ Cut 28 – 2½" x 10½" white strips.

◆ Sew the 6½" strips to opposite sides of the square and press. Add the 10½" strips to the remaining two sides. Press. *

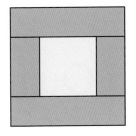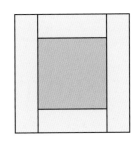

Fɪɢ. 7

Making the small blocks

There are two color variations of the smaller 5"x 5" (finished) blocks: 14 blocks with light pale pink centers framed in dark gray and 14 blocks with dark centers framed in pale pink.

◆ Make 14 blocks with pale pink centers framed in dark gray (figure 3).

    ◆ Cut 14 – 3" x 3" pale pink squares.

    ◆ Cut 28 – 1¾" x 3" dark gray strips

    ◆ Cut 28 – 1¾" x 5½" dark gray strips.

◆ Sew the 3" strips to opposite sides of the squares and press. Add the 5½" strips to the remaining two sides. Press. *

◆ Make 14 blocks with dark gray centers framed in pale pink (figure 4).

    ◆ Cut 14 – 3" x 3" dark gray squares.

    ◆ Cut 28 – 1¾" x 3" pale pink strips

    ◆ Cut 28 – 1¾" x 5½" pale pink strips.

◆ Sew the 3" strips to opposite sides of the squares and press. Add the 5½" strips to the remaining two sides. Press. *

*Alternate piecing method: I found that a quicker way to piece these blocks was to make strip-sets for the center sections (figure 5). Press, cut into sections, and add the two long strips to opposite sides to complete the block (figure 6).

If you consistently sew the blocks together so every other one is turned a quarter turn, you will avoid all the seam lines coming together and the blocks will lie flatter (figure 7).

These blocks alternate evenly in both the first smaller pieced border and the outside pieced borders. I pieced the blocks into twos and then joined them to make the borders minus the corner squares. Then it was easy to drop in the corner squares to complete the borders.

> **TIP:** This looks easy and it does go together easily *if* you sew with a consistent ¼" seam, press the seams as you go along, and pin. Pin enough so the seams line up and nothing shifts.

Minimal Quilts Inspired by Art

I began experimenting with improvisational work by making a small free-pieced Log Cabin quilt in 1987, and to this day, I work with the Log Cabin format probably more than any other. That first quilt is discussed and shown in *Liberated Quiltmaking* (page 36). Continuing to explore the idea of making abstract blocks with no pattern eventually led to what I now call Liberated quiltmaking, and with that discovery, I was off and running. A whole new world of possibilities opened up for me. A lot of my early exploration involved studying real scrappy antique quilts. Quilts like cotton crazies made me crazy to figure out what was going on and I tried to emulate them as a way to unlock their construction secrets.

I began to feel I could probably figure out how to make anything I wanted. It wasn't long before I noticed that certain painters worked in styles that were very "quilt like." For example, the work of the Dutch painter Piet Mondrian (1872–1944) was composed of simplified compositions divided in vertical and horizontal directions, and limited to a palate of primary colors along with black and white.

And so it came to pass, dear reader, that looking at Mondrian's paintings prompted me to see if I could use my techniques to do in fabric what he was doing with paint on canvas. Figuring out how to put together GEOMETRIC COMPOSITION #1 (top right) was so absorbing that GEOMETRIC COMPOSITION #2 followed close on its heels (lower right).

I had never shown anyone these two quilts because they were, after all, clearly based on Mondrian's paintings. At the time, I did think I succeeded in that they obviously bring Mondrian to mind. They definitely were a learning experience, but I saw them for what they were—exercises. So they stayed home and never went anywhere until I got a job for the Modern Quilt Guild in Ventura, California, in 2013. I took them along, showed them at my lecture, and talked about looking to modern art for ideas for modern quilts. When I held them up and asked the audience if they could tell where I got the ideas for these two quilts, a choir of people, quickly and in unison, called out "Mondrian." Yep! That was the right answer.

The best thing about the experience of diving in and making these two quilts years ago is that it started something that I have continued to do to this day—explore possible ways to put things together. Looking back at my life as a quilter, I

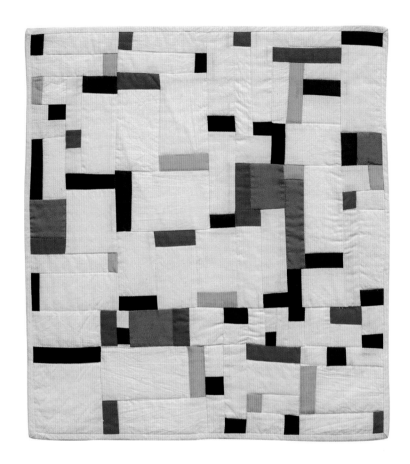

GEOMETRIC COMPOSITION #1,
17" × 19½", 1990.
Designed, made, and machine quilted
by the author.

GEOMETRIC COMPOSITION #2,
16½" × 19½", 1990.
Designed, made, and machine quilted
by the author.

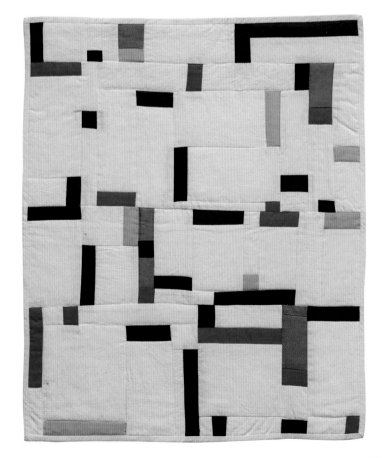

think the reason I have never, ever gotten tired of quilting, the reason I am as excited about quilting today as I was on day one, is because I discovered that I could make all sorts of quilts and I could make them my way. That's exciting and rewarding. The freedom to construct whatever comes to mind presents endless possibilities. It doesn't end ... ever.

If you start looking, you will find many parallels between paintings and quilts. That is especially true when you look at modern art and its offshoot, minimal art. Paul Klee (1879–1940) was a prolific artist and many of his pieces are very quiltlike. On a visit to the Museum of Modern Art in New York, I was inspired by his painting *Fire in the Evening* (1929) and rushed home to make UNTITLED #2 (below).

BELOW: UNTITLED #2, 18" × 18½", 1988. Wool. Designed, made, and hand tied from the back by the author. Inspired by the Paul Klee painting *Fire in the Evening* (1929).

LIBERATED PALOTA WITH APOLOGIES TO VICTOR VASARELY, 15" × 20", 2011.
Made and machine quilted by Jan Rajeck, Glen Ellyn, Illinois.

The painting measured just 13⅜" x 13¼". I can remember standing in front of it for a long time. I included this quilt in *Liberated Quiltmaking* (page 25), but that was eighteen years ago so I think it deserves another showing. Klee also did a number of paintings consisting of odd-sized squares, and I've used that idea in six or seven quilts over the years. I initially intended to include several of these quilts in this book but upon reflection realized they were really not minimal, so I had to edit myself and take them out. They were certainly Modern, but hardly minimal.

I had the pleasure of watching Jan Rajeck construct Liberated Palota with Apologies to Victor Vasarely (page 69) while at my quilt retreat in 2011. I was so impressed with it then and my delight in it has only increased since. Here is what Jan said about her quilt.

This piece is a machine-pieced tribute to "the father of op art." It is 15" x 20", the same size as his original acrylic work. The center squares were measured, but the rest of the quilt was done in a more fun and a little funky liberated style. I love this quilt in so many ways! It was created at Gwen's Beaver Island Quilt Retreat in 2011. – Jan Rajeck

Deb Albright and Kathy Sandling are good friends who share their passion for quilting. They both made quilts inspired by the work of Josef Albers. Here is Deb telling us about her piece, Interaction with Color (top right).

Gwen turned me on to Josef Albers's work and I fell in love with the simplicity of many of his studies on squares, etc. I can just visualize so many of them as quilts. I decided to take one of his works and put my favorite black and white with it. I used shot cottons because of their luminosity and put the black and white uneven stripe around the rectangles. – Deb Albright

Kathy says that when she studied Albers's work, "It was immediately apparent that his style would look amazing done in the medium of fabric." She created the illusion of overlays of rectangles and squares in her piece It's Transparent to Me (lower right).

I just loved the look of tissue paper and its transparency in some of the pieces by Josef Albers and it worked so well in fabric. The illusion of the layers of fabric showing through each other was such a reward. – Kathy Sandling

INTERACTION WITH
COLOR,
42" × 32", 2012.
Designed, made, and machine
quilted by Deb Albright,
Atascadero, California.

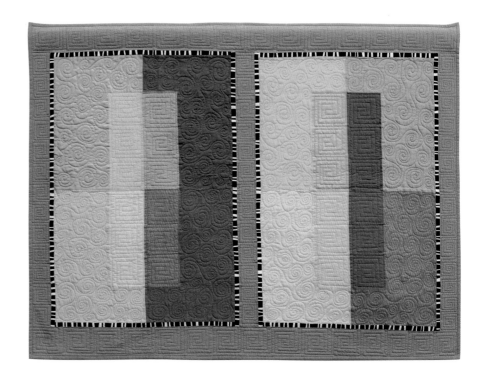

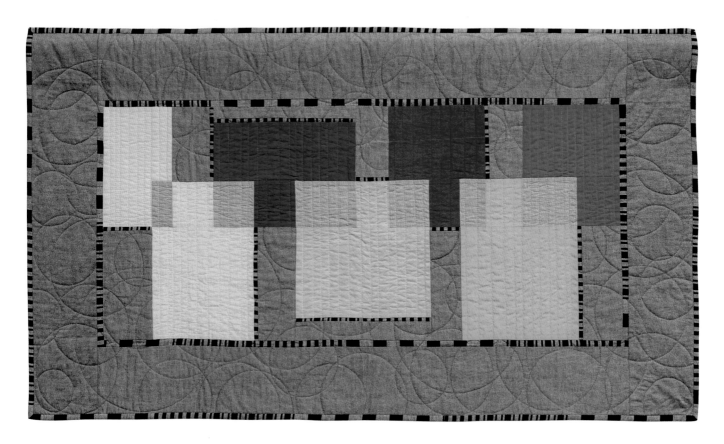

IT'S TRANSPARENT TO ME, 50" × 28", 2012. Designed, made, and machine quilted by
Kathy Sandling, Manhattan Beach, California.

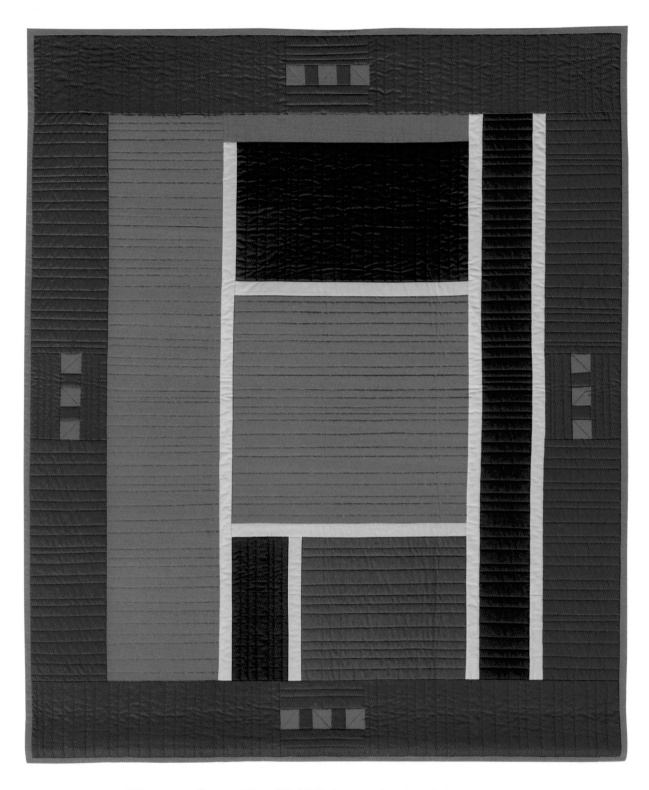

MINIMAL GRID, 56" × 67", 2013. Designed and made by the author.
Machine quilted by Rogene Fischer, Manistee, Michigan.

MINIMAL GRID (left and detail right) was again inspired by Mondrian, known for painting grids of narrow lines filled in with color. While I generally don't make such ordered work, I thoroughly enjoyed making this quilt with its clean organized look. For a strong finish, I recruited small groups of squares to stand smartly at the center of all four borders. And, I must say, I particularly like these borders. Using groups of squares as the primary decorative motif is an idea from the Scottish architect Charles Rennie Mackintosh, who is the main character in The Grand Finale: A Baker's Dozen (pages 89–93).

I worked out the design and color for this quilt by making SMALL STUDY #56 (below). With that title, you might assume I've made other small studies. Precisely! Basically I make a completed sketch in fabric, working out the color and design ideas. The sketch serves as a crystal clear map to my final destination.

SMALL STUDY #56,
9" × 10½", 2013.
Designed and made by
the author.

FIG. 1

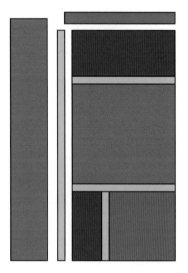

FIG. 2

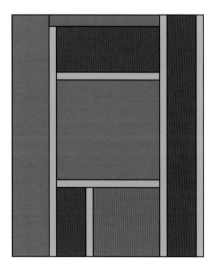

FIG. 3

MINIMAL GRID HOW-TO

While I provide the instructions and measurements (page 76) for this quilt, you might like the adventure of using the picture of the quilt as your guide and winging it for your own unique interpretation. You could play around with dividing up the sections differently, or by adding a few extra green strips to make more divisions. Or, for that matter, you could simplify the idea for an even more minimal effect.

1. Construct the three-part middle section (figure 1).

2. Add the left side border first following these 3 steps (figure 2):

◆ Sew the green strip to the right side.

◆ Add the narrow red border on the top edge of the quilt.

◆ Sew on the outer red border.

3. Sew the green strip to the right side, add the dark purple border, and add another narrow green strip to complete the inner part of the quilt (figure 3).

◆ The outer blue borders are 7" finished, so cut the long blue borders 7½" wide to include seam allowance. Once you have made the red square inserts you will be able to see how long you need to cut the blue borders, which will be sewn to either side of the inserts.

I am going to tell you exactly how I made the inserts and installed them in the border so it would fit correctly. However, it's more important that you understand the concept so you can use the idea and make it any size you want. Look at the finished insert (figure 4). This is the unit you need to construct and the trick is to oversize the long outer strips so it can be trimmed to the width of the border. If you understand the concept, you won't have to read the following instructions.

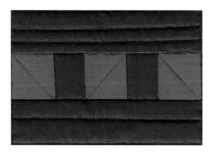

Fig. 4

Here are the steps for piecing the inserts.

1. Cut 3 red and 2 blue strips 2¼" x 10". Sew them together with the red strips on the outside (figure 5). Press.

Fig. 5

2. Cut 4 sections 2¼" wide (figure 6).

Fig. 6

3. Cut blue side pieces oversize, about 4" wide, so they can all be squared to fit the borders when sewn and pressed (figure 7). Make sure they are cut the same so the red squares will be in the same position on all four sides.

Fig. 7. Make 4.

◆ Once you have all four of the units with the red squares constructed, you are ready to insert them into the middle of the border. You will want to piece the unit with squares right in the middle of the border.

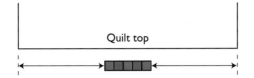

Fɪɢ. **8**. Measure for border strips.

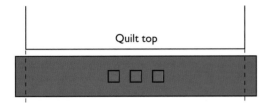

Fɪɢ. **9**. Trim to fit.

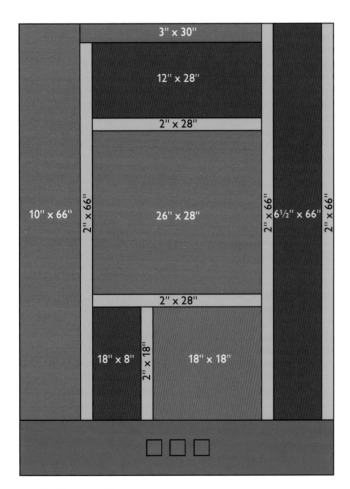

Quilt assembly

4. Lay the red square unit at the center of the quilt side. With a tape measure, see how long you need to cut the blue borders, cutting them slightly oversized to be trimmed to length later (figure 8). Sew one border on each side of the center unit. Press.

5. Find the middle of the border and the middle of the side of the quilt. With the quilt and the border lying next to each other right-sides up, measure the quilt and border. Cut the border to length (figure 9).

TIP: If you are worried you might cut the borders too short accidentally, mark the measurement you think is right, but cut the border 1" longer. Then when you put right sides together and pin the border on, pin the middle and then ends where they are supposed to be. If you discover you need another ¼" or so, you will have it.

6. With right sides together, pin the middle of the border to the middle of the quilt. Pin the ends and continue pinning the border to the quilt in sections until completely pinned. Press and square up the ends of the borders.

TIP: When you add the borders, add the sides first, and then the top and bottom. That's because if you add the top and bottom borders first, that makes the side borders really long, and therefore a bit harder to handle.

Gallery

One of the benefits of thirty plus years of my life as a traveling quilt teacher is that I've met a lot of wonderful people among whom were more than a few extraordinary quiltmakers. After all these years of visiting guilds around the country, I'm at long last releasing my findings in this brief report.

In almost every guild I visit I have the pleasure of meeting quilters who are just as accomplished, if not more so, as most of us "quilt professionals." At my own quilt retreat, which I had for thirty years, I got to know many excellent quilters and also made lifelong friends. To summarize, I can report that there are a lot of very fine quiltmakers sprinkled about. This book offers the opportunity to introduce a little handful of them to you.

Pat Isaman is a quilt teacher and quiltmaker extraordinaire from Harrodsburg, Kentucky. I am very fond of her work. She came to my quilt retreat in recent years and worked on quilts I liked so much that I found myself wishing I had created them. Her work usually involves more complicated construction, and, while she confessed to finding working with the limits implied by minimal construction to be challenging, I think she rose to the occasion. Both GARDEN FENCE (page 78) and SUMMER STORM (page 79) are made with hand-dyed fabrics by Cherrywood and were machine pieced and machine quilted by Pat.

Here is what Pat says about GARDEN FENCE.

> *I was thinking about looking across my iris fields in mid-April when the flowers are all in bloom and swaths of color show through the fence. – Pat Isaman*

And here she is talking about SUMMER STORM.

> *I was listening to the news talking about the storms in the area and started thinking about the lightning strikes that often come with summer storms. I tried to represent the heat of summer and the lightning. – Pat Isaman*

LIBERATED SHIRTINGS (page 80) was made by Kathleen Awalt from Baltimore, Maryland. She made it at my quilt retreat in 2009. I remember well that it was a big hit with all the other quilters there—shirting fabrics and small scraps, sewn together intuitively, translated into an uncontrived and heartwarming quilt.

GARDEN FENCE, 20½" x 28", 2013. Designed, made, and machine quilted
by Pat Isaman, Harrodsburg, Kentucky.

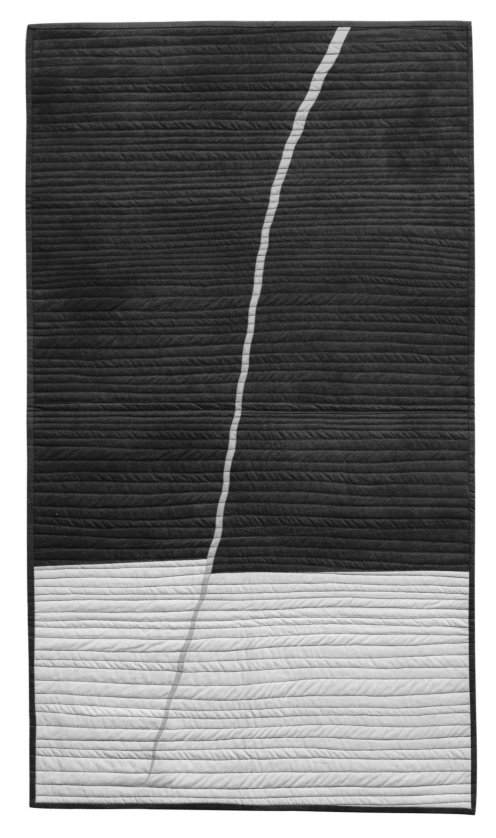

SUMMER STORM, 20¼" × 34½", 2013. Designed, made, and machine quilted
by Pat Isaman, Harrodsburg, Kentucky.

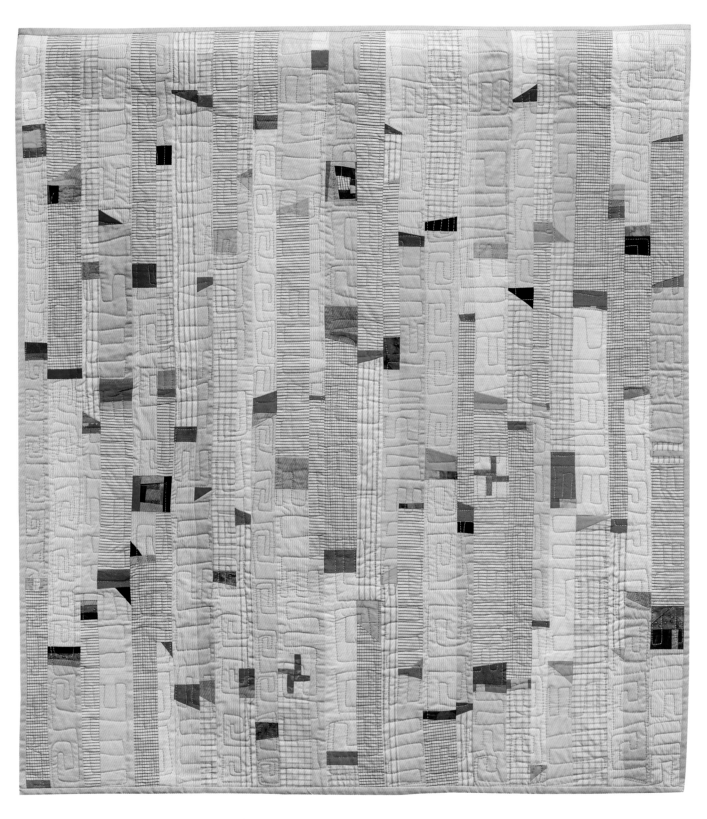

LIBERATED SHIRTINGS, 39½" x 43", 2009. Designed, made, and
machine quilted by Kathleen Awalt, Baltimore, Maryland.

FROM THE COPPER COUNTRY (upper right) was designed and made by Pam J. Beal and Wayne Walma. This small study features a large circle print, a vintage Japanese Yukata cotton. The other materials in this piece reflect Pam and Wayne's location in Michigan's Upper Peninsula, an area known for its copper mining history, rich mineral deposits, hard maple, and the Lake Superior Circle Tour.

Here is Pam talking about this piece.

Framed art quilts are a result of collaboration with my husband, Wayne Walma. We enjoy this work and our pieces have won several awards in regional art shows. Jurors and the audience alike express pleasant surprise at the interaction of cloth and wood, and appreciation for the complexity and detail of the pieces.
– Pam J. Beal

Pam and Wayne's work is represented by Blue Heron Gallery in Elk Rapids, Michigan; Artistree Gallery in Land O' Lakes, Wisconsin; and Great Lakes Trading Company, Silver City, Michigan. You can find them on their blog at: *www.overthefencedesignsgallery.blogspot.com.*

ONTONAGON CLAY (lower right) was one of Pam's first adventures with minimal design and restrained color.

CIRCLE TOUR (page 82) is the larger quilt that expands upon the small study. Making random cuts in the large circle print and working Log Cabin-style allowed the circle to dance around. The random lines of hand quilting add texture to the quiet background.

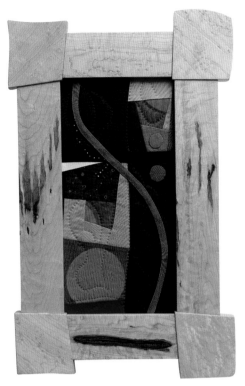

FROM THE COPPER COUNTRY, 11" × 17" × ¾", 2012. Designed and made by Pam J. Beal and Wayne Walma. Mass City, Michigan. Hand quilted by Pam. Made with cotton and bird's eye maple with mineral stain, copper, and glass beads.

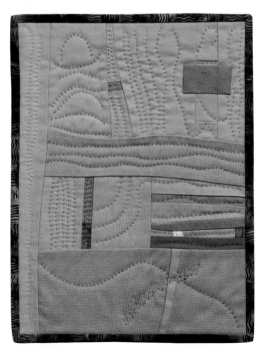

ONTONAGON CLAY, 9" × 11½", 2011. Designed, made, and hand quilted by Pam J. Beal, Mass City, Michigan.

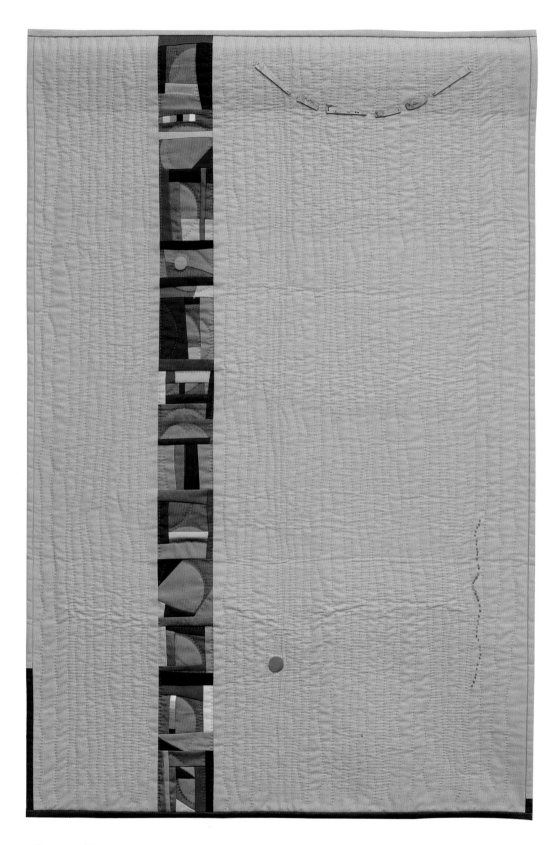

CIRCLE TOUR, 28" x 41", 2012. Designed, made, and hand quilted in a floor frame by Pam J. Beal, Mass City, Michigan.

Phyllis Small is an established art quilter from West Hartford, Connecticut. Here, she talks about her quilts and her ideas about minimal work.

In CHOPSTICKS (page 84), I used a large negative gray space with two narrow lines of color. I felt that the added interest of spiral quilting was necessary to finish the piece. I did not want to add another element of a binding so I finished it with a facing. GREEN AND ORANGE (page 84) was made with a lime green background and contrasting line elements that are repeated in the quilting.

My idea of a minimal quilt is one which is sparse, large or small, but with few elements. That could mean one or two shapes, a large negative space, or few colors or lines. In experimenting with my own idea of minimal quilts, I had trouble finding the right balance. My quandary was to simplify my compositions, which can tend to get complicated, and at the same time keep them interesting. I like both more and less, and I struggled to satisfy both urges. – Phyllis Small

THE FIRE IN MY BACK (page 85) was made by Pat Haas. Here is what Pat says about making this quilt.

I love working with squares because the piecing is simple and it allows me to concentrate on the design and color of the quilt. Designing is my favorite part of making a quilt and the color selection and placement is mentally challenging and exciting. I love solids and my hand dyeds. I don't use many print fabrics because I find them somewhat distracting. The simplicity of pure color is my underlying esthetic.

As I began putting the green blocks together, I was finding the result to be boring, so I inserted some reddish orange behind the blocks and it created a glow. The glow factor is something I love to achieve. It still wasn't enough, so I started rummaging through my parts drawer and found the black-and-white segment. As I pinned it on the board it reminded me of a beautiful line drawing of a spinal cord that I had recently seen. It looked great with the green blocks and was just the extra spark that the quilt needed. I inserted a few other black lines for continuity. The fire-like glow of the orange behind the blocks, the spinal cord, and my aching back led to the title of the quilt. I randomly straight-line machine quilted it with red and green rayon thread. – Pat Haas

And here Pat tells us about THE HORIZON AT VIEUX FORTE (page 85).

About twelve years ago a friend of mine vacationed in St. Lucia and took the photo that was the inspiration for this small quilt. I was fascinated with the periwinkle color of the sky and the blue green of the water. The fabric for the water is one of my hand dyeds. I hand quilted this small quilt to simulate the calm sky and the ripple and sparkle of the water. – Pat Haas

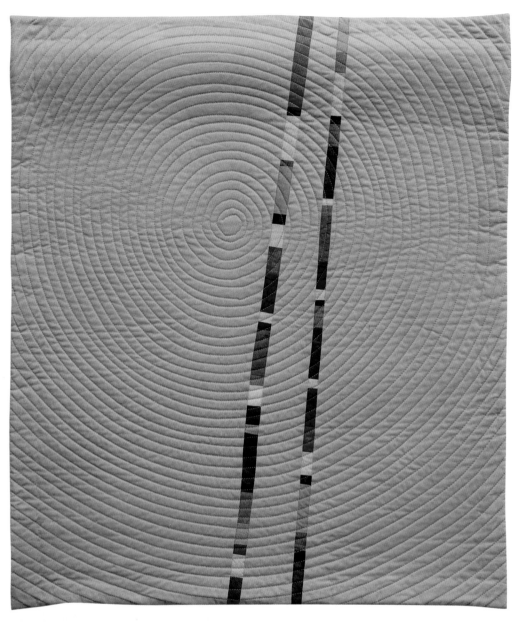

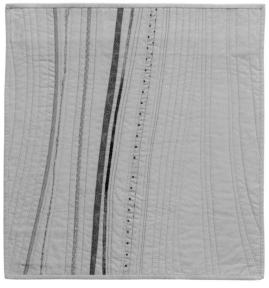

ᴀʙᴏᴠᴇ: **Cʜᴏᴘsᴛɪᴄᴋs,** 24" × 28", 2013.
Designed, made, and machine quilted by Phyllis Small,
West Hartford, Connecticut.

ʟᴇғᴛ: **Gʀᴇᴇɴ ᴀɴᴅ Oʀᴀɴɢᴇ,** 18½" × 18¾", 2012.
Designed, made, and machine quilted by Phyllis Small,
West Hartford, Connecticut.

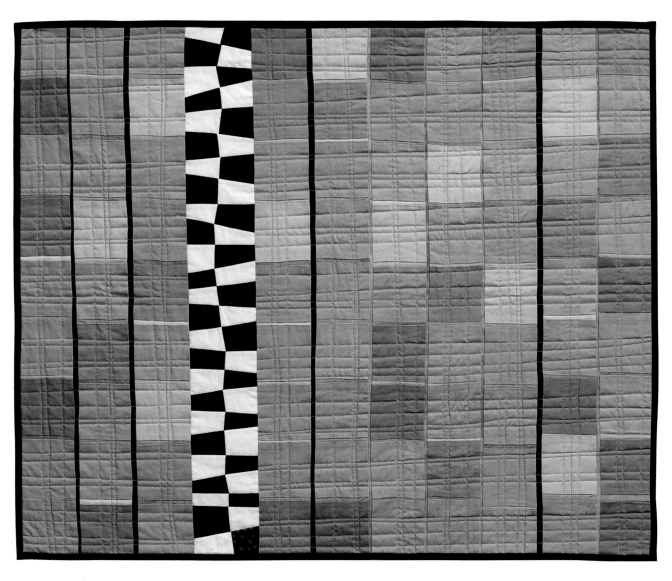

ABOVE: **THE FIRE IN MY BACK,** 34" × 28", 2013. Designed, made, and machine quilted by Pat Haas, Annapolis, Maryland.

RIGHT: **THE HORIZON AT VIEUX FORTE** 12" × 12", 2013. Designed, made, and hand quilted by Pat Haas, Annapolis, Maryland.

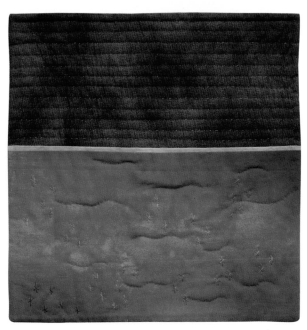

Deb Albright hails from sunny California. She is an avid quiltmaker and here is what she says about GEOMETRIC DELIGHT (below).

This quilt was going to be the back of a liberated quilt I made in Gwen's class at Asilomar in 2012. I liked it so much that it became a quilt. It was a very organic experience using big chunks of fabric and letting my intuition take me along. The circles came last as it just needed something, and when I auditioned them, they did the trick. The quilting is done on my longarm and is all free motion, which is another aspect of quilting that I love.
– Deb Albright

GEOMETRIC DELIGHT,
43" x 44", 2012.
Designed, made, and machine quilted by Deb Albright, Atascadero, California.

ENTROPY, 47" × 59", 2013. Designed, made, and machine quilted by Elisa Albury, Salt Lake City, Utah.

I know Elisa Albury from her days as editor for *Quilter's World* magazine as well as other quilt books and pattern books and as one of the regulars at the Beaver Island Quilt Retreats. She has recently written articles for national quilt magazines and has had designs published in several books. She also writes about quilts on her blog, *Stitch Outside the Ditch* (www.stitchoutsidetheditch.com). Elisa has recently started teaching classes in an effort to spread the word about liberated quilting techniques as well as share new ways to look at our fabric stash.

Here is what Elisa told me about her quilt ENTROPY (above).

As a quilter, I don't typically work in a minimal style, so this quilt was a great challenge for me. In addition, I feel like the word "minimal" is subject to many interpretations. In this design I chose to explore the concept of working with minimal ingredients. I used three elements: unbleached muslin combined with the smallest of scraps all set with the simplest of units—the humble square. These scrap bits are the leftovers I have as a result of the way I have been processing fabric. I like that this quilt is simultaneously chaotic yet structured. The squares create a sense of order—a fabric representation of expansion and contraction.
– Elisa Albury

I like ending this section with a quilt made by a friend who has been quilting for just three years; through her love and dedication for the art form, she seems to be breathing down the necks of those of us who have been quilting for many more years. Nice work, Barbara!

INDIGO CURVES, 30" × 30", 2013. Designed, made, and machine quilted by Barbara Mars, Milwaukee, Wisconsin, using Cherrywood fabrics with linen/cotton inserts.

The Grand Finale:
A Baker's Dozen

n 1990, I started what would quickly become a series of minimal pieces motivated by images of Charles Rennie Mackintosh's designs that I ran across in *Architectural Digest*. The article showed pictures of a Mackintosh interior, so stunning that they prompted me to put down the magazine and pick up my needle.

Mackintosh (1868–1928) was a brilliant Scottish designer who was well ahead of his time. His clean architectural designs, interiors, and furniture designs were progressively modern and in sharp contrast with the fussy Victorian style of his day. He created his own unique style by combining the elements of the English Arts and Crafts and Art Nouveau movements with the Scottish vernacular with which he was obviously familiar.

The images in *Architectural Digest* showed a bedroom with both the walls and furniture painted white. The only decorative motifs in the room were a grouping of nine pink squares in an arrangement of three across and three down, gracing the closet doors, the bed, and the dressers. The starkness of nine squares against all that white transformed something that was elementary and understated into something quite extraordinary. It was absolutely striking, elegant, and sophisticated.

I decided I'd make a small white quilt with one pink square centered near the top, then cover it with as spectacular quilting designs as I could muster. One quilt wasn't enough to satisfy my interest in combining minimal piecing and maximum quilting, and eventually there were thirteen—a baker's dozen.

Because of my unbridled enthusiasm to explore multiple design ideas, and because of the time it takes to hand quilt complicated designs, these quilts by necessity were also minimal in size. They all measure 18" x 20". Eleven of them were made in 1990, and five years later I did two more pieces, which spoke of a little garden I maintained in a hard-to-discover location, though close to my house. Weather permitting, I could wander out there with my morning coffee and welcome the day.

ONE PATCH, 18" × 20", 1990. Designed, made, and hand quilted by the author.

Except for ORANGE PEEL (upper right, page 91), quilted with the teacup design, and CRAZY ONE-PATCH II (lower right, page 91), quilted in diamonds, they are quilted with variations of traditional Welsh designs. I've long been enthralled with Welsh quilting designs for their uniquely distinctive style. Starting out as a hand quilter, quilting designs have always interested me. I spent a lot of time in my early years studying quilting designs, figuring out how to draft them, and how to get the designs onto the quilt. In those early heady years, I thought I knew a lot about quilting designs, and I actually did. But when I finally saw examples of Welsh quilting, I realized that I was seeing entirely different ideas expressed in the quilting stitch.

While American quilting designs are very beautiful, the Welsh designs, also beautiful, are completely different and I set out to learn about them. This series of small, minimal quilts became an ideal canvas upon which to explore the language of Welsh quilting design.

Before I leave this subject, I'd like to encourage you to look up Charles Rennie Mackintosh on the web. Today, he is to Glasgow what Gaudi is to Barcelona. The story of his personal life, his brilliant wife and partner, Margaret MacDonald, and the watercolors he painted late in life are so worth learning about. Investigate the Room de Luxe at the Willow Tearooms, designed with his wife in the Art Nouveau style for which they are famous. A quick Internet search will bring up multiple images, including his chairs, complete with nine pink squares. Better still, stop by for tea the next time you are in Glasgow.

ABOVE: Room de Luxe at the Willow Tearooms.

RIGHT: Charles Rennie Mackintosh

OFF-CENTER SQUARE, 18" × 20", 1990.
Designed, made, and hand quilted by the author.

ORANGE PEEL 18" × 20", 1990.
Designed, made, and hand quilted by the author.

CRAZY ONE-PATCH I, 18" × 20", 1990.
Designed, made, and hand quilted by the author.

CRAZY ONE-PATCH II, 18" × 20", 1990.
Designed, made, and hand quilted by the author.

BLUE AND RED ONE-PATCH, 18" × 20", 1990.
Designed, made, and hand quilted by the author.

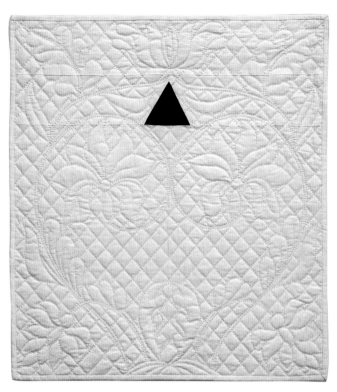

BLACK TRIANGLE, 18" × 20", 1990.
Designed, made, and hand quilted by the author.

PINK TRIANGLE, 18" × 20", 1990.
Designed, made, and hand quilted by the author.

PURPLE TRIANGLE, 18" × 20", 1990.
Designed, made, and hand quilted by the author.

BLUE SPRUCE, 18" × 20", 1990.
Designed, made, and hand quilted by the author.

NINE-PATCH, 18" × 20", 1990.
Designed, made, and hand quilted by the author.

GWEN'S SECRET GARDEN I, 18" × 20", 1995.
Designed, made, and hand quilted by the author.

GWEN'S SECRET GARDEN II, 18" × 20", 1995.
Designed, made, and hand quilted by the author.

About the Author

Gwen Marston has spent over thirty years as a professional quiltmaker, author, and teacher. She is perhaps best known for the Liberated quiltmaking methods she developed that enable quilters to do their own original work by using an intuitive approach to design. Instead of a pattern, Gwen uses a process to make the parts of the quilt. She has taught nationally and internationally; her articles have appeared in many magazines in the states and elsewhere; and she offered quilt retreats in northern Michigan near her home for thirty years. This is her twenty-seventh book.

In addition to writing and teaching, Gwen has had twenty-eight solo exhibits of her larger work and seven exhibits of her small quilts.

ABOVE: TURQUOISE, detail. Full quilt on page 47.

RIGHT: Photo by Sue Weston, taken at Gwen's exhibit, Taupo Museum, Taupo, New Zealand

Other Books by Gwen Marston

37 Sketches. Six Mile Creek Press, 2011. An award winner at the 2012 New York Book Show

70 Classic Quilting Patterns: Ready-to-Use Designs and Innovations (with Joe Cunningham). Dover Publications, Inc., 1987.

American Beauties: Rose and Tulip Quilts (with Joe Cunningham). AQS Publishing, 1988.

Amish Quilting Patterns: 56 Full-Size Ready-to-Use Designs and Complete Instructions (Dover Quilting) (with Joe Cunningham). Dover Publications, Inc., 2011.

Classic Four-Block Applique Quilts: A Back-to-Basics Approach. C&T Publishing, 2010.

Collaborative Quilting: Talking It Over (with Freddy Moran). Sterling/Chapelle, 2006.

Fabric Picture Books. AQS Publishing, 2002.

Freddy and Gwen Collaborate Again: Freewheeling Twists on Traditional Quilt Designs (with Freddy Moran). Lark Books, 2009.

Gwen Marston's Needlework Designs. AQS Publishing, 2006.

Ideas and Inspirations: Abstract Quilts in Solids. MoCa Press, 2008.

Liberated Medallion Quilts. AQS Publishing, 2012.

Liberated Quiltmaking. AQS Publishing, 1996.

Liberated Quiltmaking II. AQS Publishing, 2009.

Liberated String Quilts. C&T Publishing, 2010.

Lively Little Folk-Art Quilts: 20 Traditional Projects to Piece & Appliqué. C&T Publishing, 2006.

Mary Schafer and Her Quilts (with Joe Cunningham). Michigan State University Press, 1991.

Mary Schafer, American Quilt Maker. The University of Michigan Press/Regional, 2004. Awarded a 2005 Notable Book Award by the Michigan Library Association.

Q Is for Quilt: An ABC Quilt Pattern Book. Michigan State University Press, 1987.

Quilting with Style: Principles for Great Pattern Design (with Joe Cunningham). AQS Publishing, 1993.

Sets and Borders (with Joe Cunningham). AQS Publishing, 1987.

Twenty Little Amish Quilts: With Full-Size Templates (Dover Quilting). Dover Publications, 1993.

Twenty Little Four-Patch Quilts: With Full-Size Templates (Dover Quilting). Dover Publications, 2012.

Twenty Little Log Cabin Quilts: With Full-Size Templates (Dover Quilting). Dover Publications, 1995.

Twenty Little Patchwork Quilts: With Full-Size Templates (Dover Quilting) (with Joe Cunningham). Dover Publications, 1990.

Twenty Little Pinwheel Quilts: With Full-Size Templates (Dover Needlework). Dover Publications, 1994.

Twenty Little Triangle Quilts: With Full-Size Templates (Dover Needlework). Dover Publications, 1997.

other AQS books

This is only a small selection of the books available from the American Quilter's Society. AQS books are known worldwide for timely topics, clear writing, beautiful color photos, and accurate illustrations and patterns. The following books are available from your local bookseller, quilt shop, or public library.

#1418 . . . .$26.95

#8763 . . . .$24.95

#1423 . . . .$24.95

#1421 . . . .$24.95

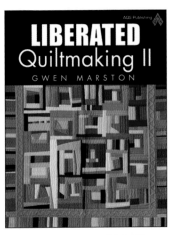

#8147 . . . .$28.95

#8150 . . . .$24.95

#8665 . . . .$19.95

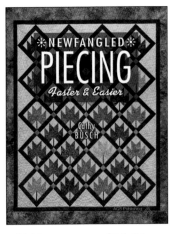

#1420 . . . .$24.95

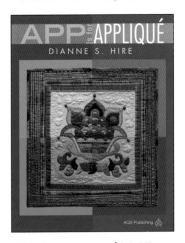

#1419 . . . .$24.95

LOOK for these books nationally.
CALL or **VISIT** our website at

1-800-626-5420
www.AmericanQuilter.com